ANNOTATED
TEACHER'S

READING
COMPREHENSION
WORKSHOP

MOMENTUM

GLOBE FEARON
EDUCATIONAL PUBLISHER
PARAMUS, NEW JERSEY

Paramount Publishing

Executive Editor: Virginia Seeley
Senior Editor: Bernice Golden
Editor: Lynn W. Kloss
Editorial Assistant: Roger Weisman
Product Development: Brown Publishing Network
Art Director: Nancy Sharkey
Production Manager: Penny Gibson
Production Editors: Nicole Cypher, Eric Dawson
Marketing Manager: Sandra Hutchison
Photo Research: Jenifer Hixson
Electronic Page Production: Siren Design
Cover Design: Carol Anson
Cover Illustration: Jennifer Bolten

Globe Fearon Educational Publisher wishes to thank the following copyright owners for permission to reproduce copyrighted selections in this book: **Margaret Walker Alexander**, for Margaret Walker "Lineage" from *Jubilee* by Margaret Walker (New Haven: Yale University Press, 1942). **Dial Books for Young Readers, a division of Penguin Books USA Inc.**, for Nicholasa Mohr, excerpt from *Going Home*. Copyright (©) 1986 by Nicholasa Mohr. And for Mildred D. Taylor, excerpt from *Let the Circle Be Unbroken*. Copyright (©) 1981 by Mildred Taylor. **Doubleday, a division of Bantam Doubleday Dell Publishing Group, Inc.**, for Greg Cohoe "Thirst" from *The Whispering Wind: Poetry by Young American Indians* by Terry Allen. Copyright (©) 1972 by the Institute of American Indian Arts. **Mari Evans and Reed Visuals**, for Mari Evans "The Alarm Clock." **Victor Gollancz Ltd.**, for Mildred D. Taylor, excerpt from *Let the Circle Be Unbroken*. Copyright (©) 1981 by Mildred Taylor. **GRM Associates, Inc., Agents for the Estate of Ida M. Cullen**, for Countee Cullen "Incident" from *Color* by Countee Cullen. Copyright (©) 1925 by Harper & Brothers; copyright renewed 1953 by Ida M. Cullen. **Margaret K. McElderry Books, an imprint of Macmillan Publishing Co.**, for Yoshiko Uchida, excerpt from *Journey Home*. Text (©) 1978 Yoshiko Uchida. **Dr. D. H. Melhem**, for D. H. Melhem "Grandfather: Frailty Is Not the Story" from *Grape Leaves: A Century of Arab American Poetry* by Gregory Orfalea and Sharif Elmusa. Copyright (©) 1988 by University of Utah Press. **Gregory Orfalea**, for H. S. Hamod "Leaves" from *Grape Leaves: A Century of Arab American Poetry* by Gregory Orfalea and Sharif Elmusa. Copyright (©) 1988 by University of Utah Press. **Simon J. Ortiz** for Simon Ortiz "My Father's Song" from *Harper's Anthology of 20th Century Native American Poetry*, edited by Duane Niatum. **Leroy Quintana**, for Leroy Quintana "The Legacy II" from *Grandparents' Houses*. (©) 1984 Greenwillow Books. **The Estate of Yoshiko Uchida**, for Yoshiko Uchida, excerpt from *Journey Home*. Text (©) 1978 Yoshiko Uchida. **The Westminster Press / John Knox Press**, for Maureen Crane Wartski, excerpt from *A Long Way Home*. Copyright (©) 1980 Maureen Crane Wartski.

Globe Fearon Educational Publisher wishes to thank the following copyright owners for permission to reproduce illustrations and photographs in this book: **p. 9**: Photograph, M. Bryan Ginsberg; **p. 11**: Illustration by David Tamura; **p. 15**: Illustration by David Tamura; **p.45**: Photograph, courtesy of Laura Weber; **p. 50**: Photograph, Focus On Sports; **p. 66**: Photograph, AP/World Wide Photos; **p.86**: Photograph, Lawrence Migdale, Stock Boston; **p. 91**: Photograph, courtesy of Detroit Institute of the Arts; **p. 107**: Photograph, Laura Lehrhaupt; **p.108**: Photograph, courtesy of General Motors Corporation; **p. 109**: Photograph, courtesy of Chevrolet Public Relations; **p. 116**: Illustration by Siren Design; **p. 144**: Illustration by Siren Design; **p. 146**: Illustration by Siren Design.

Printed in the United States of America   3 4 5 6 7 8 9 10 99

ISBN: 0-835-90588-8

GLOBE FEARON
EDUCATIONAL PUBLISHER

PARAMUS, NEW JERSEY

Paramount Publishing

CONTENTS in Order of Skill Presentation

Overview   **T6**
List of Workshop Skills *Reflections, Momentum,* and *Perspective*   **T8**
Contents by Cultural Group *Reflections, Momentum,* and *Perspective*   **T10**
Model Graphic Organizers   **T11**

Unit One Becoming an Active Reader: Novel Excerpts   1

Model Selection from *Going Home* by Nicholasa Mohr   8
Review Selection from *A Long Way From Home*
  by Maureen Crane Wartski   12

Lesson 1   **Point of View**
    Introducing   2
    Practicing   3
    Applying   4
    Reviewing   16
    Testing   17

Lesson 2   **Context Clues**
    Introducing   5
    Practicing   6
    Applying   7
    Reviewing   18
    Testing   19

Unit Two Becoming an Active Reader: Novel Excerpts   20

Model Selection from *Journey Home* by Yoshiko Uchida   27
Review Selection from *Let the Circle Be Unbroken* by Mildred Taylor   29

Lesson 3   **Making Inferences**
    Introducing   21
    Practicing   22
    Applying   23
    Reviewing   32
    Testing   33

Lesson 4   **Sensory Language**
    Introducing   24
    Practicing   25
    Applying   26
    Reviewing   34
    Testing   35

Unit Three Becoming an Active Reader: Newspaper Articles   36

Model Selection *Laura Weber: One Native American Whose Business
  is the Environment* by Janice Gay   43
Review Selection *The Alomars—Baseball's Version of All in the
  Family* by Arturo and Maureen Gonzalez   47

Lesson 5   **Compare and Contrast**
    Introducing   37
    Practicing   38

          Applying   39
          Reviewing   52
          Testing   53

Lesson 6   **Key Words**
          Introducing   40
          Practicing   41
          Applying   42
          Reviewing   54
          Testing   55

Unit Four Becoming an Active Reader: Magazine Articles   56

Model Selection *Gloria Estefan: Her Remarkable Recovery*
  by Fernando Romero   63
Review Selection *Rap Music: What's it All About?* by Ron Harris   68

Lesson 7   **Main Idea and Details**
          Introducing   57
          Practicing   58
          Applying   59
          Reviewing   73
          Testing   74

Lesson 8   **Fact and Opinion**
          Introducing   60
          Practicing   61
          Applying   62
          Reviewing   75
          Testing   76

Unit Five Becoming an Active Reader: Encyclopedia Entries   77

Model Selection *Kwanzaa* by Naurice Roberts   84
Review Selection *Diego Rivera* by Mary Lou Nevarez Haugh   88

Lesson 9   **Reading an Encyclopedia Entry**
          Introducing   78
          Practicing   79
          Applying   80
          Reviewing   93
          Testing   94

Lesson 10   **Classifying Words**
          Introducing   81
          Practicing   82
          Applying   83
          Reviewing   95
          Testing   96

Unit Six Becoming an Active Reader: How-To Articles   97

Model Selection *How-To Buy a Used Sports Car* by Brian Alexander   104
Review Selection *How To Make Tasty, Nutritious Recipes with Beans*
  by Julie Catalano   110

Lesson 11   **Sequence**
          Introducing   98
          Practicing   99

Applying   100
Reviewing   117
Testing   118

Lesson 12   **Cause and Effect**
Introducing   101
Practicing   102
Applying   103
Reviewing   119
Testing   120

Unit Seven Becoming an Active Reader: Poems   121
Model Selection *The Alarm Clock* by Mari Evans   128
Review Selections *My Father's Song* by Simon J. Ortiz   129
Grandfather: Frailty Is Not the Story by Diana H. Melhem   130

Lesson 13   **Sound and Meaning**
Introducing   122
Practicing   123
Applying   124
Reviewing   132
Testing   133

Lesson 14   **Analogies**
Introducing   125
Practicing   126
Applying   127
Reviewing   134
Testing   135

Unit Eight Becoming an Active Reader: Poems   136
Model Selections *Leaves* by H. S. Hamod   143
Thirst by Gary Cohoe   145
Review Selections *Lineage* by Margaret Walker   146
Incident by Countee Cullen   147

Lesson 15   **Cultural Context**
Introducing   137
Practicing   138
Applying   139
Reviewing   148
Testing   149

Lesson 16   **Author's Tone**
Introducing   140
Practicing   141
Applying   142
Reviewing   150
Testing   151

Book Test Part 1 Fiction   152
Book Test Part 2 Nonfiction   154

OVERVIEW

INTRODUCTION

The goal of *Reading Comprehension Workshop* is to help students become skilled **active readers**. As they complete the lessons, students interact with the text by applying skills and strategies. Each *Workshop* lesson helps students become aware of the natural reading process by learning what skilled readers "see" as they read for understanding. **Skills and strategies** that are central to the *Workshop*, such as Cause and Effect, Main Idea and Details, and Author's Purpose, are described in a way that clarifies why and how they can be used to read actively. A graphic organizer visually demonstrates each skill and strategy.

Reading Comprehension Workshop develops **critical thinking skills** that help students make connections between old ideas and new. It shows them how to find new information and to utilize prior knowledge. Through the *Workshop*, students discover how to respond to literature. They respond by discussing and writing about their thoughts and ideas as well as how the text makes them feel. Through active participation, students learn to slow down the reading process so that they can see it "one frame at a time." Students learn to take control of their reading by rereading for clarification, visualizing for understanding, and responding to what they read.

The **multicultural literature** selected for the *Workshop* is original and not adapted. The below-grade reading levels and high-interest content of the selections are appropriate for improving readers and for **ESL/LEP** students. Fiction and nonfiction genres are equally represented; all literature within a unit is taken from the same genre. In addition, units are paired by genre.

Reading Comprehension Workshop also prepares students for state **reading proficiency tests**. All skills included in the workshop reflect state standards in the language arts and reflect testing terminology, format, and procedures.

A Walk Through a Unit

As you glance at the table of contents, you will notice that the student text is divided into units. Each unit begins with a **Unit Opener** and contains two lessons and two multicultural literature selections. As you page through a unit, you will see that the lessons follow a logical plan. This plan provides a page in each lesson for **Introducing, Practicing,** and **Applying** each of the lesson skills before the literature selections, and **Reviewing** and **Testing** after the selections.

As you can see, a **Lesson Bar** (on page 2, for example) appears across the top of each lesson page. Notice how the lesson bar shows the student the page on which each part of the lesson appears. Note that the words *Introducing, Practicing, Applying, Reviewing,* and *Testing* match the sequence of lesson components mentioned above.

Arrow Guides also direct students through each unit. If you turn to page 4 of the student text (the first Applying page of the book), you will see an arrow, which will direct you to the Reviewing page for that lesson. Arrow guides direct students from lesson pages to selection pages.

The two literature selections within each unit are adjacent to one another. The **Model Selection**—the first of the two literary works—is used to introduce and provide practice for both lessons in the unit. The **Review Selection** is used to review and test the skills and strategies in both lessons.

Workshop Features

Unit Openers Openers introduce the genre and encourage students to become active readers. You can use this feature to let students know why the skills and strategies presented in the unit are useful and to discuss how culture is reflected in the genre of the unit's selections. You can also use this feature to help students make connections between the reader's response to literature and the writing of sidenotes.

Level	Title	Reading/ Interest Level	Genres
Book 1	Insights	3/6	Folktales, Myths, Short Stories, Poems, Articles
Book 2	Crossroads	4/7	Short Stories, Biographies, Autobiographies, Speeches, Essays
Book 3	Reflections	5/8	Short Stories, Articles, Essays, Poems
Book 4	Momentum	6/9	Novel Excerpts, Newspaper Articles, Magazine Articles, Encyclopedia Articles, How-to Articles, Poems
Book 5	Perspective	7/10	Short Stories, Editorials, Plays, Humorous Essays, Persuasive Essays
Book 6	Spectrum	8/11	Novel Excerpts, Short Stories, Letters. Advertorials, Encyclopedia Articles, Poems, Songs, Reference Articles, Encyclopedia Articles

Model and Review Selections The Model and Review Selections were carefully selected for their diverse cultural voices. Since the interest level of the literature is high, you can use it to motivate students to read, discuss key issues, and apply the skills and strategies. The nonfiction fosters a critical view of ideas; the fiction encourages a comparison of new and known ideas.

Sidenotes Sidenotes show how one reader responded while reading. They also model how that reader applied the lesson skill and strategy to the selection. Space is provided in the margins for students to write their own sidenotes for both the Model Selection and the Review Selection. Students might need several practice sessions writing sidenotes as they actively become involved in the reading process.

Graphic Organizers In every lesson, the Introducing page presents a graphic organizer that shows students the process of applying the skill and strategy being taught. Students use the graphic organizers to apply the skill and strategy to the unit selections.

Writing Activities Students are given many opportunities to increase their comprehension skills through writing. A writing prompt appears in Section B of every Practicing, Applying, Reviewing, and Testing page. These writing activities develop the students' critical thinking skills and allow them to express their own ideas about key issues presented in the selections. Brief writing activities appear on every Introducing page, allowing students to respond to the sidenotes. In addition, students comment in writing about their answers to test items.

Assessment The two **Testing** pages in each unit and the **Book Tests** at the end of the book are geared toward the state proficiency tests. Various testing formats are included: cloze, multiple choice, true-false, and fill-in-the-blanks. In addition, more than one answer is sometimes correct. Students must support each answer with a written statement explaining their reasoning.

ANNOTATED TEACHER'S EDITION

The *Reading Comprehension Workshop Annotated Teacher's Edition* provides you with suggested student answers and teacher annotations at point of use. It also gives you options for extending the lesson.

Student Answers

Many of the questions in the program are open-ended, allowing for a range of answers. The same is true of the writing activities and the graphic organizers. However, the *Workshop ATE* provides model answers and suggestions for responses to questions, writing activities, and graphic organizers. Use the modeled Student Answers to assess students' responses. Keep in mind that a student's answer is acceptable if he/she can support it with adequate evidence from the selection or from prior knowledge.

Teacher Annotations

Three types of Teacher Annotations, which are positioned in the margins, provide you with a variety of support systems. General Annotations appear throughout the program. Page-Specific Annotations appear on the same pages throughout the ATE. Assessment Annotations suggest alternative ways to assess students' work.

General Annotations General Annotations that provide suggestions for developing the language skills of students acquiring English appear as **ESL/LEP** annotations. These annotations focus on dramatization, visual interpretation, and oral language development. **Peer Sharing, Individualized Learning**, and **Cooperative Learning** annotations provide recommendations for grouping students. **Writing Process** and **Conferencing** annotations provide suggestions for expanding student writing and guiding students' responses to each other's writing.

Page-Specific Annotations Each ATE Introducing page begins with the **Lesson Objective,** which shows you an approach for **Modeling the Strategy,** and gives pointers for **Managing the Lesson**.

The Practicing page of the ATE clarifies the **Purpose** of the page and explains how students can use the strategy in the graphic organizer to complete the page.

The ATE Applying page provides suggestions for **Applying the Skill to Other Media, Applying the Skill to Everyday Reading**, or **Applying the Skill to Other Disciplines.**

Annotations on the first Literature page include **Preteaching Vocabulary, Motivating Question, Accessing Prior Knowledge,** or **Making Predictions**, each of which promotes student interaction with the text before reading. While the student is reading, annotations highlight **Additional Skills, Cultural Awareness,** and **Meeting Individual Needs**, each of which focuses on the special needs of students. In addition, a **Clarification** annotation offers students the opportunity to clarify their understanding of the selection.

Annotations that provide **Response Clues** suggest ways that students might apply the skill to the selection through writing sidenotes and marking text by circling, underlining, and drawing arrows. Note that the Response Clues and marks within the text are suggestions, since there are no required responses.

The annotations on the Reviewing page give suggestions for **Reviewing the Strategy**. Annotations on the **Testing** page include **Test-Taking Hints**.

Assessment Annotations Assessment Annotations provide alternative guidelines to measure student learning. These include **Student Self-Assessment, Assessing Cooperative Work, and Assessing Student Writing**.

LIST OF WORKSHOP SKILLS

Reflections, Momentum, Perspective

UO = Unit Opener　　L = Lesson　　Boldface = Lesson Title *in Momentum*			

COMPREHENSION	Book 3 Reflections	Book 4 Momentum	Book 5 Perspective
Drawing conclusions	UO2　L3		
Compare and contrast	UO4,6 L7	UO3 L4,5,15	UO 2,3,4,8
Main idea and details	UO4, L8	UO4, L7	UO3
Cause and effect	UO6, L11	UO6, L12	UO6,8, L15
Making inferences		UO2, L3	UO2, L3
Predicting outcomes		L5	UO6, L11
Fact and opinion		UO4, L8	UO4, L7
Sequence		UO6, L11	UO2, L4
CRITICAL THINKING			
Responding to various forms of literature	applied throughout the series		
Visualizing characters, events, and setting	UO1	UO2,6	UO5
Using prior knowledge/personal experience		L12	
• to understand what is read	UO2,4	UO3,4,8	UO2,6
• to make inferences		UO2	L3
• to predict outcomes	UO3		UO6, L11
• to determine sequence		L11	
Recognizing similarities and differences	L7	UO3,8, L5	L13
Recognizing how point of view affects response		UO1, L1	UO1, L1
Recognizing how setting affects characters and events		UO2, L3	
Responding to statements of fact and opinion		L8	L7
Making judgments			L4,5,7,8
Responding to key words in an editorial			L6
Evaluating persuasive writing			UO4,8, L8,15
Summarizing			UO8, L16
GENRE AND AUTHOR'S CRAFT			
Plot	UO1, L1		UO5, L9, 12
Story conflict	UO1, L1		
Problem and solution	UO2, L4		UO6, L12
Reading			
• **encyclopedia articles**		UO5, L9	
• editorials			UO3, L5

• humorous essays			UO7, L13
• nonfiction	UO3, L5, 7		
• plays			UO6
Author's viewpoint	UO5, L9		
Author's purpose	L9	L16	UO4, L5
Speaker of a poem	UO7, L13		
Mood	UO7,L14		
Point of view		UO1, L1	UO1, L1
Sensory language		UO2, L4	
Sound and meaning		UO7, L13	
Author's tone		UO8, L16	
Persuasive techniques			L8
Humorous techniques			UO7, L13
APPRECIATING DIVERSITY			
Recognizing similarities and differences among cultures	UO1,5, L12	UO1	UO3
Developing understanding and tolerance towards others	UO1		UO8
Recognizing diversity within a culture	UO2,5		
Appreciating one's heritage	L6		L6, 14
Cultural context	UO6, L12	UO6,8, L2,15,16	
Recognizing cultures' common values	UO7	UO8	UO5
Recognizing authors' cultural perspectives		UO2, L15	UO8
Gaining insight into cultural traditions			UO1
VOCABULARY			
Context clues	UO1,5, L2,10,11	UO1, 2,7	UO1,7, L2,10,12,14
Idioms	UO1, L2		
Key words	UO3, L6	UO3, L6, 10	UO3, L6
Synonyms and antonyms	L10	UO1	L14
Identifying words			
• that show cause and effect	L11	L12	
• that show opinions or judgments		L8	
• that signal sequence		L11	
• that signal analogies		UO7, L14	
Analogies		UO7, L14	
Classifying words		UO5, L10	
Multiple meaning words			UO1, L2
Pronouns			UO5, L10

T 9

CONTENTS by Cultural Group

This list shows the cultural background of the authors whose selections appear in *Reflections, Momentum,* and *Perspective.*

African and African American
Thank You, M'am by Langston Hughes   **Reflections   14**
The Beginnings of Art in Africa by Helena St. Louis (Trinidadian)   **Reflections   49**
What's in a Name? by Lindamichellebaron   **Reflections   81**
An African's Adventures in America by Babs Fafunwa   **Reflections   101**
Poetry Lesson Number One by Wanda Coleman   **Reflections   114**
from *Let the Circle Be Unbroken* by Mildred Taylor   **Momentum   29**
Rap Music: What's It All About? by Ron Harris   **Momentum   68**
Kwanzaa by Naurice Roberts   **Momentum   84**
The Alarm Clock by Mari Evans   **Momentum   128**
Lineage by Margaret Walker   **Momentum   146**
Incident by Countee Cullen   **Momentum   147**
There Are Lots of Reasons for African Americans to Be Upbeat
   by Donald E. Winbush   **Perspective   65**
A Change of Heart by Darwin McBeth Walton   **Perspective   79**
Barbara Jordan: The Beauty Within Us by Brenda Lane Richardson   **Perspective   86**
The Strange Case of My Brother, or The Saturday Mystery by Jerdine Nolen Harold   **Perspective   101**

Asian and Asian American
from *A Long Way from Home* by Maureen Crane Wartski (Japanese American)   **Momentum   12**
from *Journey Home* by Yoshiko Uchida (Japanese American)   **Momentum   27**
Stop Stereotyping Asians by Catherine Yi-yu Cho Woo (Chinese American)   **Perspective   62**
Why Asians Should Play Asian Roles by Angela Chen (Chinese American)   **Perspective   146**

Latino
The No-Guitar Blues by Gary Soto (Mexican American)   **Reflections   8**
Gabriela's Game by Guadalupe J. Solis, Jr. (Mexican American)   **Reflections   31**
Stowaway by Armando Socarras Ramírez (Cuban American)   **Reflections   97**
from *Going Home* by Nicholasa Mohr (Puerto Rican)   **Momentum   8**
The Alomars—Baseball's Version of All in the Family
   by Arturo and Maureen Gonzalez (Mexican American)   **Momentum   47**
Gloria Estefan: Her Remarkable Recovery
   by Fernando Romero (Mexican American)   **Momentum   63**
Diego Rivera by Mary Lou Nevarez Haugh (Mexican American)   **Momentum   88**
How To Make Tasty, Nutritious Recipes with Beans
   by Julie Catalano (Mexican American)   **Momentum   110**
from *Amigo Brothers* by Piri Thomas (Puerto Rican)   **Perspective   8**
What Can Be Learned from Latino Political Gains
   by Leonel Sanchez (Peruvian American)   **Perspective   46**
Why Homemade Tortillas Are a Thing of the Past
   by Frank Moreno Sifuentes (Mexican American)   **Perspective   129**

Native American
Little Bighorn: A Native American Perspective by Darryl Babe Wilson (Pitt River)   **Reflections   84**
Laura Weber: One Native American Whose Business Is the Environment
   by Janice Gay (Hupa)   **Momentum   43**
My Father's Song by Simon J. Ortiz (Acoma)   **Momentum   129**
Thirst by Grey Cohoe (Navajo)   **Momentum   145**
Preserving Native American Culture Should Be a National Concern
   by Rick Hill (Tuscarora)   **Perspective   49**
Why and How the BIA Should Be Dissolved by Darryl Babe Wilson (Pitt River)   **Perspective   143**

European American
Sarah Tops by Isaac Asimov (Jewish American)   **Reflections   29**
Cuban Americans Today by Deborah A. Parks (German American)   **Reflections   46**
The Facts About Skin Cancer by Kristi Jogis (Scandanavian American)   **Reflections   62**
Estonia Returns to Life by Elin Toona Gottschalk (Estonian American)   **Reflections   66**
Gaining Yardage by Leo Dangel   **Reflections   116**
How To Buy a Used Sports Car by Brian Alexander (Scottish American)   **Momentum   104**
An Ordinary Woman by Bette Greene (Jewish American)   **Perspective   12**
Lemmings by Richard Matheson   **Perspective   28**
Tank by Francis Izzo   **Perspective   30**
The Heritage Project by Elaine Epstein (Jewish American)   **Perspective   109**
Shark Treatment by Dave Barry   **Perspective   126**

Middle Eastern
Grandfather: Frailty Is Not the Story by Diana H. Melhem (Lebanese American)   **Momentum   130**
Leaves by H.S. Hamod (Lebanese American)   **Momentum   143**

Name _____ Date_____

Point of View: Circle the words that tell you who is telling the story. On the chart below, record how point of view affects your responses to the story.

Question ➤	Look Back ➤	Respond
Who's telling the story? Which words tell me this? _____ _____ _____ _____ _____ _____ _____	What are some thoughts and feelings expressed by the main character? OR What are some story events that are described by an outside narrator? _____ _____ _____ _____	How did the point of view affect my response to the story? _____ _____ _____ _____ _____ _____

- -

Name _____ Date_____

Making Inferences: Combine selection clues with what you already know to make inferences. Write your responses for one inference in the puzzle pieces below.

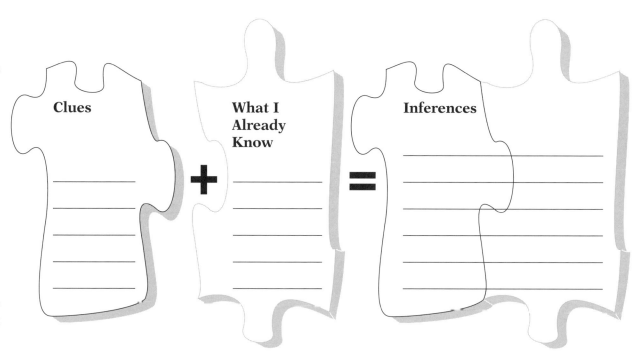

Clues

+

What I Already Know

=

Inferences

Name _____ **Date**_____

Author's Tone: Underline details that show the author's tone in the selection. Then use your responses in the diagram below to analyze the author's message.

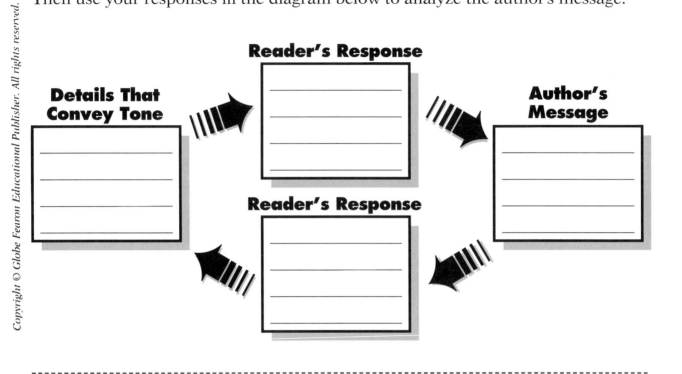

Name _____ **Date**_____

Cause and Effect: As you read the selection, circle the causes you find and draw arrows to their effects. Use your findings in the chart below.

CAUSE	EFFECT
CAUSE	EFFECT
CAUSE	EFFECT

Name _____ **Date** _____

Context Clues: When you read an unfamiliar word or phrase in another language, look for context clues to its meaning. Write these clues on the checklist below.

Question	Yes	No	If yes . . .
Are there story clues or author clues that help me identify the other language?	☐	☐	Identify the language. _____ _____
Can I find a word or words that mean about the same or the opposite of the unfamiliar word?	☐	☐	Write the word or words. _____ _____

- -

Name _____ **Date** _____

Compare and Contrast: Noting similarities and differences can help you see ideas or characters more clearly. Write your observations on the Venn diagram below.

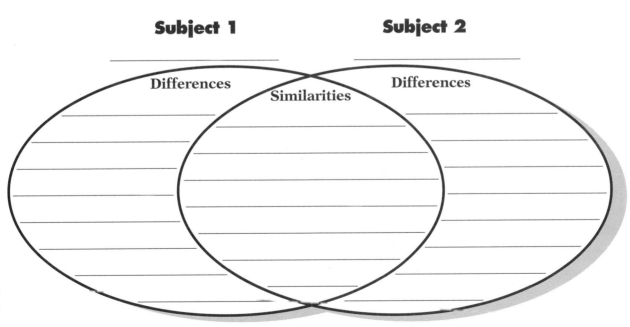

Subject 1   **Subject 2**

Differences   Similarities   Differences

Name _____ **Date** _____

Main Idea and Details: After reading the selection, underline the main ideas and circle the details that support them. Record your findings for one main idea on the wheel below.

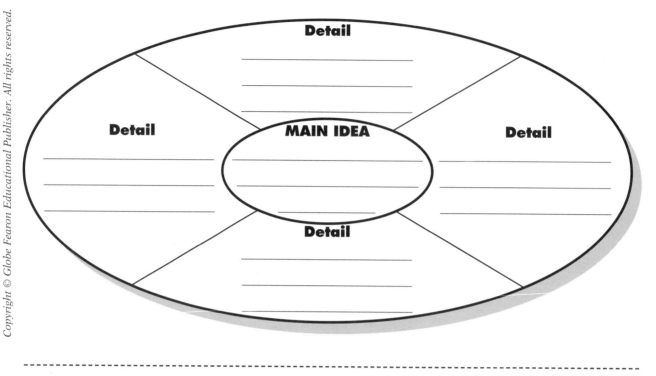

- -

Name _____ **Date** _____

Fact and Opinion: As you read, make notes about the facts and opinions you find. Use this information in the chart to analyze your responses to three statements in the selection.

Statement	Is It Fact or Opinion?	Reader's Response to Statement
Statement 1: _____ _____	_____ _____	_____ _____
Statement 2: _____ _____	_____ _____	_____ _____
Statement 3: _____ _____	_____ _____	_____ _____

T 14

Name _____   **Date**_____

Classifying Words: In the cluster below, write three categories of words from the selection. Then write words that fit into these categories on the small ovals.

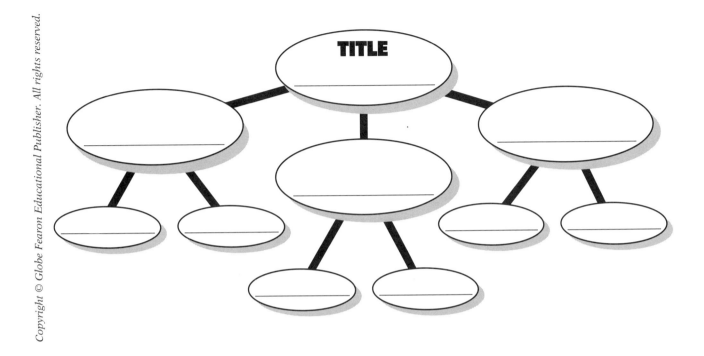

- -

Name _____   **Date**_____

Reading an Encyclopedia Article: As you read, note how what you *already know* and what you *want to know* affects what you learn. Record your responses on the chart below.

What do I already know the topic?	What do I want to know?	What have I learned from reading the entry?
_____	_____	_____
_____	_____	_____
_____	_____	_____
_____	_____	_____
_____	_____	_____
_____	_____	_____

Name _____ Date_____

Sequence: Circle the signal words you find in the selection and draw arrows that show the order of events. Use these notes to outline sequence on the chart below.

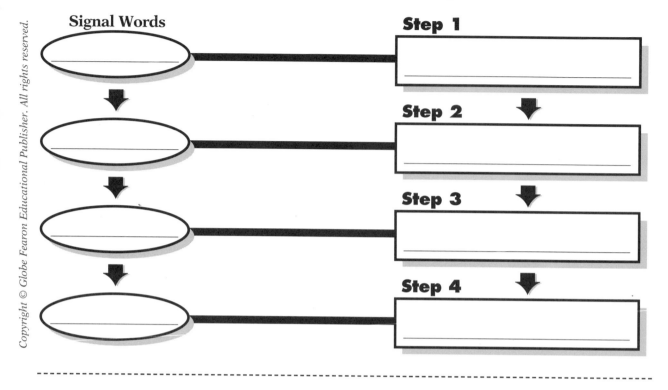

Signal Words

Step 1

Step 2

Step 3

Step 4

- -

Name _____ Date_____

Cultural Context: Fill in the diagram below with details about the author's life, the cultural clues in the selection, and your background. Then write your response to the selection.

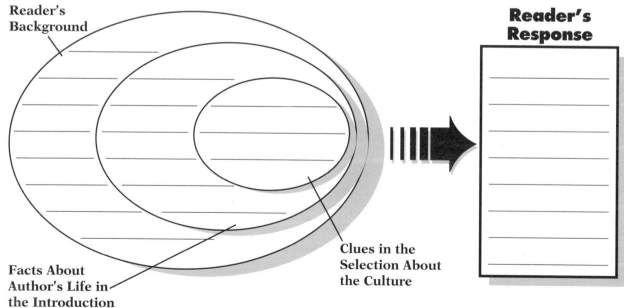

Reader's Background

Reader's Response

Facts About Author's Life in the Introduction

Clues in the Selection About the Culture

T 16

Unit ONE

BECOMING AN ACTIVE READER

Reading **novel excerpts** actively means becoming involved with the characters. Good readers join in story conversations, judge characters' actions, and give characters advice. A good reader often feels like a character's best friend.

Using Skills and Strategies

Asking questions about a novel's **point of view** can help you become involved with its characters. You might look back and ask: Who's telling this story? What thoughts and feelings is the character describing? Would I respond differently if another character told the story?

Using **context clues** to figure out words from another language can also help you become involved in a story. To understand these words, you might ask: Are there clues that can help me identify the language? Can I find words that mean the same as or are the opposite of the unfamiliar words?

In this unit, identifying **point of view** and using **context clues** will help you become a more active reader.

The Novel Excerpt: The Writer's Voice

The diversity of our country is reflected in its novels. Through a novel's characters, authors from many cultures describe unique experiences of the people in those cultures. You will gain many insights reading novels by authors from diverse cultures. As you read, you will learn about cultural differences, but you will also learn that people from all cultures are alike in many ways.

Responding to Novels

When reading a novel excerpt, readers might question how it fits into the novel plot line. In this unit, it is important to note your responses to the excerpts from *Going Home* and *A Long Way from Home*. Use your notes to discuss the excerpts with your classmates.

Unit Enrichment: Invite students to write a diary entry for one of the story characters. Have them write about the character's feelings and reactions to events that happened during the time period described in the novel excerpt. Remind students that diary entries are written in the first-person point of view. Have available classroom copies of the two novels excerpted in this unit, *Going Home* and *A Long Way From Home*.

Point of View

| Lesson 1 | Introducing page 2 | Practicing page 3 | Applying page 4 | Reviewing page 16 | Testing page 17 |

Introducing Strategies

Point of view lets the reader know who is telling the story. Sometimes a story is written in the first person. The storyteller, or **narrator**, is one of the characters. Here is an example: *I said goodbye bravely.* An author may also write a story in the third person. The story is told by an outside narrator. Here is an example: *He said goodbye bravely.* In first-person stories, narrators usually focus on their own thoughts and feelings. In a third-person story, the outside narrator reveals the thoughts and feelings of many characters. In this way, the reader's response is affected by the narrator's point of view.

The chart below shows how readers question, look back, and respond to point of view while reading.

Question	Look Back	Respond
Who's telling the story? Which words tell me this?	Can I identify examples of thoughts and feelings expressed by the main character? **OR** Can I identify story events described by an outside narrator?	How did the point of view affect my response to the story?

Reading the Novel Excerpt

Read the excerpt from *Going Home* on pages 8-11 and the sidenotes on pages 8-9. These notes show how one good reader reacted to point of view. Then complete the items below.

1. How does the reader know this story is written in the first-person point of view?

The word *I* in *I lay in bed* and *"all I can think of"* tells the reader that the story is told
_____
in the first person.

2. List some ways this point of view affected the reader's response to the story and the characters.

The reader felt close to the narrator because she expressed her thoughts and feelings.
_____
The reader felt as if the narrator were a friend.

Practicing **Point of View**

A. Circle the letter of the choice that best completes each sentence below. Then, on the lines provided, explain why you selected that answer.

1. First-person point of view helped the reader *mostly* to

    a. see the story and characters through Gigi's words.

    b. get to know Vinny.

    (c.) find out Felita's thoughts and feelings.

    d. both b and c above.

The first-person point of view tells the thoughts and feelings of the narrator, Felita.

_____

2. If the author had used third-person point of view, the reader

    a. might not have known what was behind Felita's conversation with Gigi on Saturday.

    b. might not have found out Felita's feelings about Vinny.

    (c.) both a and b.

    d. neither a nor b.

If the excerpt were in the third person, Felita's personal thoughts and feelings both

about Vinny and Gigi might not be evident.

3. In this story, first-person point of view helps the reader feel

    a. like an outsider.

    (b.) close to the narrator

    c. like an intruder.

    d. lonely.

The first-person point of view gives readers a personal insight into one character.

_____

B. Write a paragraph about an incident that happens between a main character and his or her best friend. Use either the first-person or the third-person point of view.

Accept all appropriate responses. Responses should clearly indicate that students

recognize how the first-person point of view or the third-person point of view

is written.

_____

_____

_____

Purpose: The purpose of this page is to help students practice the skill of identifying point of view in a novel excerpt. Items reflect the question, look back, respond strategy shown in the graphic organizer on the **Introducing** page.

Peer Sharing: Have students complete Section A independently. Then invite them to work with a partner to compare answers. Encourage students to make sure their partners give details from the story to support their responses.

Conferencing: For part B, invite small groups of students to read their paragraphs aloud to each other. Ask students to tell how their responses written in the first person were different from those written in the third person.

ESL/LEP: Students whose knowledge of English is still limited may wish to write the paragraph in their first language. You can then help them rewrite the paragraph in English.

Applying *Point of View*

Applying the Skill to Other Media: Discuss how point of view affects students' responses to other media, such as popular TV programs. A suggestion for discussion is the first–person narration in "Wonder Years." Ask students for additional examples.

Individualized Learning: Have students complete the page independently. Make sure that they give explanations for their answers in Section A.

ESL/LEP: Have students reread the passage aloud, converting the third-person narration to first–person. Have students work with partners whose first language is English.

A. Read the paragraphs below and think about the point of view. Then answer the questions that follow.

> *Elena took a deep breath and stood up tall before entering the classroom. She knew going to a new school would be hard, but she never imagined she would be this nervous. Her hands shook as she opened the classroom door and walked in. A thousand strange eyes seemed to look up at her. Then she heard a cheerful voice call out, "Welcome!"*
>
> *Mrs. Santana, Elena's new teacher, was smiling and motioning to a desk where Elena could sit. As a young girl, Mrs. Santana had moved from school to school herself. She knew exactly how Elena was feeling at this moment.*

1. Are the events in these paragraphs written in the first-person or the third-person point of view? List some words from the paragraphs that helped you decide.

Paragraphs are written in the third-person point of view. The paragraphs include use of

words such as *she* and *her*, and they tell how both Elena and Mrs. Santana feel.

2. How did the point of view affect how you responded to the characters and the incident described? List some of the ways.

Accept all appropriate responses. Students may suggest that third-person narration

doesn't allow them to hear how Elena was feeling from her own point of view.

Writing Process: You may wish to have students develop their paragraphs into short stories. They can use their response as the first paragraph in the story, or as a stimulus for story ideas.

B. Write a short paragraph describing someone who is in a new situation. Use either the first-person or the third-person point of view. Check to be sure that your point of view stays the same throughout the paragraph.

An understanding of the skill and strategy of the lesson should be reflected in the

writing activity. Do narrators in first-person paragraphs reflect their own thoughts

and feelings? Do narrators in third-person paragraphs describe story events as *they*

see them?

To review

↓

page 16

Context Clues

Introducing Strategies

Sometimes authors bring the flavor of their own cultures into the stories they write. One way they do this is to have the characters use words from the language spoken by people of that culture.

Good readers use **context clues** to help them figure out the meanings of words from other languages. Context clues are words in the same sentence or in nearby sentences that help the reader define unfamiliar words.

Here's a checklist of questions that good readers ask themselves in order to understand words from other languages by using context clues.

Questions	Yes	No	If yes . . .
Are there story clues or author clues that help me identify the other language?			Identify the language.
Can I find a word or words that mean about the same or the opposite of the unfamiliar word?			Write the word or words.

Reading the Novel Excerpt

Reread the excerpt from Going Home on pages 8-11. On page 8 the story says, "How I wished my grandmother was alive . . . Mami would never understand. But my _abuelita_ would have . . ."

1. From which language is the word _abuelita?_ What story clues tell you this?

Clues from the introduction, the title _Going Home,_ and the words "my trip to

Puerto Rico" and "my Spanish reader" suggest that _abuelita_ is a Spanish word.

2. Is there a word in a nearby sentence that means the same as the word _abuelita?_ What does _abuelita_ mean?

In the previous paragraph the word _grandmother_ means about the same as the

Spanish word _abuelita._

Lesson Objective: To use a checklist strategy to identify context clues to figure out the meaning of words in excerpts from the novels _Going Home_ and _A Long Way from Home._

Oral Language: Write the word _mañana_ on the chalkboard and explain that it is a Spanish word meaning "tomorrow." Invite students to use the word in sentences in which they use context clues that help define what the word means.

ESL/LEP: Encourage students to use the strategy for using context clues to help them figure out the meanings of English words as well.

Modeling the Strategy: Have available a passage from a familiar story or novel that uses words in other languages. Read the passage aloud and model using context clues to figure out the meaning of foreign words. Refer to the questions in the checklist. Use the Reproducible Activity Master on page T13 of the ATE to help students apply the strategy to the excerpt from _Going Home._

Meeting Individual Needs: If necessary, help students use story clues to answer these two questions.

Practicing **Context Clues**

A. The sentences below are from the novel *Going Home*. Circle the letter of the choice that best completes the statement. Then tell why you selected each answer.

1. "Tío bought me a vanilla cake with pineapple icing that had been decorated with the words **BUENA SUERTE** GOOD LUCK, FELITA!"

The English term _____ probably has the same meaning as the Spanish term *buena suerte*.

    a. *vanilla cake*   c. *pineapple icing*
    b. *decorated*   (d.) *good luck*

The words *GOOD LUCK* follow the words *BUENA SUERTE* on the cake.

2. "Why, oh, why did she have to die? Why couldn't it have been **Tío** Jorge instead of her? Right after I thought this, I felt guilty and I spoke out loud. 'Forgive me, Abuelita, I really didn't mean it. I know how much you love Tío . . .'"

In Spanish, *Tío* probably is a name for a _____.

    a. greeting   c. feeling
    (b.) relative   d. command

Tío preceeds a proper name. Felita says her abuelita loves Tío.

3. "'Mami? Say it's okay. Please, please?'"
"'**Bueno** . . . okay.'" My mother heaved a big sigh.

In this passage, the Spanish word *bueno* is used to mean the English word _____.

    a. *please*   (b.) *okay*
    c. *mother*   d. *sigh*

Mami says the word *okay* immediately after saying *Bueno*.

B. Write a paragraph in which you use two words from another language or two made-up words. Give context clues that will help readers figure out the meanings of both words.

Students' paragraphs should include an appropriate context clue for each of the

unfamiliar words that they use.

_____

_____

_____

Applying **Context Clues**

A. The passages below are from Nicholasa Mohr's *El Bronx Remembered*. For each item, first circle clues to the meaning of the word in bold type. Then answer the questions.

1. " 'Hi, man, How you doing?' "
   " '(What's happening,) baby?' "
   " '*Qué pasa,* man?' "

Look at how *qué pasa* is used. Does it name a food, offer a greeting, or give an order? How can you tell?

Qué pasa offers a greeting. It is used in response to the greeting "What's happening?"

and probably means about the same thing.

2. " 'Yvette, you wanna have some *matzo?* We got some for the (holidays.)' "
   " 'Is that the (cracker) they gave you this afternoon?' "
   " 'Yeah. You can have some.' "

What does *matzo* mean? How do you know?

Matzo is a cracker eaten on the Jewish holiday of Passover. The first speaker mentions

the holidays. "Is that the cracker...?" is answered in the affirmative.

B. Each passage below contains a word from another language. Use context clues to help you rewrite each passage, substituting an English word for the foreign word.

1. "This *shillelagh* may look like a big old stick to you, but my grandfather once used it in Ireland to defend himself."

Sample: This club may look like a big old stick to you, but my grandfather once used

it in Ireland to defend himself.

2. "I have to dust mom's collection of little glass figurines. I get so bored wiping the dust off all those *chachkas.*"

Sample: I have to dust mom's collection of little glass horses. I get so bored wiping

the dust off all those knick-knacks.

C. Reread the sentences in each item above. Do you think anything was gained by using the word from another language? What was lost?

Accept all appropriate responses. Students should address what was lost or gained in

each example when they substituted a word from another language.

Applying the Skill to Other Disciplines: As students read social studies texts or other class assignments, encourage them to write sidenotes on notebook paper to illustrate how they use context clues to figure out the meaning of words from other languages.

Peer Sharing: Have students complete Section A with a classmate. Encourage both partners to explain why they responded as they did.

Individualized Learning: Have students complete Section B independently. Students can then compare the English words they used in their sentence with the words that their classmates used.

Cultural Awareness: Point out that *Qué pasa* is a Spanish term, *matzo* and *chachkas* are words in Yiddish, and *shillelagh* is an Irish word. Invite students to name other words from languages that are part of their heritage or culture.

To review

page 18

Preteaching Vocabulary:
You may wish to preteach the following vocabulary words: *El Barrio, delirious, Fort Knox, privileges, Europe, customs.*

Motivating Question: As students read the excerpt from *Going Home*, ask them to think about what the author might be saying about how traditions, beliefs, and customs affect the lives of the story characters.

The notes in the margins on pages 8 and 9 show how one reader thought about point of view while reading.

The story says, "I lay in bed" and "all I could think of." It's probably being told in the first-person point of view.

Meeting Individual Needs:
Reluctant readers tend to read or become involved in reading as little as possible. Have students read the sidenotes on pages 8 and 9. Then ask them to underline the text that supports the sidenotes they have read. This will help develop a growing responsibility for reading involvement.

The narrator is telling me her thoughts and feelings directly. I'll look for some more of the narrator's thoughts and feelings as I read.

The narrator is like a friend, telling me about feeling guilty and wishing her grandmother were alive.

Meeting Individual Needs:
For students who find sidenotes confusing, have them fold back the page and read the selection without the model sidenotes.

Nicholasa Mohr (1935-   ) was born in El Barrio, a New York City neighborhood whose people are mostly of Puerto Rican descent. Much of her writing deals with life in El Barrio, especially the struggles of the people to adjust to city life and a new culture. In *Going Home*, Felita, the main character, takes Spanish lessons and has a crush on the boy giving those lessons.

from Going Home

by Nicholasa Mohr

. . . Later that night as I lay in bed, trying to study the grammar in my Spanish reader, all I could think of was Vinny. When Vivian had made her nasty remarks that afternoon, I was embarrassed because I like Vinny so much. Lately even my trip to Puerto Rico had seemed less important than being with him. In fact I could hardly wait for Mondays and Thursdays so we could have our lessons and be together. I was getting to like him as much as I liked Gigi, only it was different. When I am with Gigi, I feel secure and happy because I know I can share all my secrets with her, and she will always understand. With Vinny, I get this feeling of excitement like I wanna put my arms around him and give him a big hug. Just looking at the way he laughs or puts his head over to one side makes me feel great. We don't even have to talk! Sometimes just being in the same room with him makes me feel delirious with joy! But I'm also worried. What if he doesn't feel the same way?

How I wished my grandmother was alive so I could talk to her. I just couldn't help wondering why my getting older had to make things so complicated. When I was little, life was a lot simpler. But now my brothers were in charge of me. Mami watched me like I was the gold in Fort Knox and someone was gonna steal me! Plus I knew now that I wanted Vinny to be my boyfriend. Was this wrong?

Mami would never understand. But my abuelita would have, and she would have told me what to do. She would help me and together we could figure all this out. Why, oh, why did she have to die? Why couldn't it have been Tio Jorge instead of her? Right after I thought this, I felt guilty and I spoke out loud. "Forgive me, Abuelita, I really didn't mean it. I know how much you love Tio and I love him too, honest. It's only that right now I'm so

confused and I miss you something fierce." Tears came to my eyes because really I didn't want Tio to die. I know how much he loves all of us. All I wanted was for Abuelita to come back to me.

The only person I could talk to was Gigi. So I decided to feel her out, introduce the subject and see what she thought. Maybe she could tell me if what I felt was right, if I had a chance with Vinny or was way off base. No matter what, I knew I could trust her.

That next Saturday when Gigi and me sat in her room, listening to her cassette player, I brought up the subject of Vinny, trying to sound real casual.

"Gi, do you think Vinny likes Vivian?"

"What? Are you crazy? He doesn't even look her way."

"Oh, I thought maybe you had observed something about him that I didn't."

"What I observed about Vinny Davila ain't got nothing to do with Vivian."

"You mean he might like someone else?" I asked.

"He sure does."

I turned my eyes away from Gigi. "Who do you think she is?"

"Come on, Felita,"—Gigi caught my eye and smiled—"don't be telling me you don't know."

"I don't!" I kept on pretending I didn't know what she meant.

"You know he likes you. Admit it, Felita. And you like him too." That's all I wanted to hear. I couldn't keep a straight face anymore.

"Oh, Gigi, you're right. I'm really crazy about him. I just hope he likes me the same way."

ESL/LEP: Students whose first language is not English may wish to share names for *mother, father, aunt, uncle, grandmother,* and *grandfather,* in their native languages.

Additional Skills: This selection is also appropriate for identifying character traits and characters' feelings. Ask if students think the dialogue makes the characters seem believable.

◀ It seems I know the narrator really well because she's told me her thoughts and feelings. I even know what's behind this conversation with Gigi.

◀ As the narrator, I wonder if she is going to tell Gigi's thoughts too.

Write your own sidenotes as you read the rest of the story. In your notes, focus on how point of view affects your response to the story.

Response Clue: The conversation between Felita and Gigi may lead students to understand that because Gigi is seen through the eyes of Felita, readers can't fully understand Gigi's private thoughts and feelings.

Response Clue: Students might recognize that the first-person point of view gives them insight into Felita's feelings about her family.

Clarification: You may wish to have students stop at this point and review events to help them understand that even though a direct conversation is taking place, the novel excerpt is still told in the first person.

Additional Skills: This section of the excerpt is also appropriate for teaching the skill, Cultural Context (see ATE page 137).

"I think you will be Vinny's girl. And it's gonna happen soon."

"Wow. I hope so. If he asks me to be his girl, he's getting a loud YES!" We hugged. I could tell Gigi was real happy for me. "There's only one big problem if that happens, though, and that's Mami. If she knew how I felt about Vinny, she'd kill me and stop the lessons for sure."

"So just make sure she doesn't find out. Act real cool, and don't say a word to her."

"I guess so. You know what really burns me up? My brothers can get away with murder and nobody says anything to them. For instance, Tito can come in the house and say that some girl has fine legs, or is really built, and my parents just laugh. Like it's all so funny, right? Me, I wouldn't dare say a word about Vinny. They say I'm wrong to feel I should be treated like my brothers. Gi, do you think I'm wrong to feel like that?"

"No, you're absolutely right, Felita. You should be equal to your brothers. You're even smarter than them. They can't draw like you, right? Why should boys get more privileges than girls just because they are boys? Doris told me that if I had a brother, we'd be treated the same."

"You're so lucky, Gigi. I wish Mami could be like Doris. It's not that I don't love Mami, because I know she does care for me, but I never can talk to her. She doesn't believe I have problems. I mean it! She thinks I have this perfect life."

"I know I'm lucky because Doris doesn't treat me like most P.R. mothers treat their daughters. She's more modern."

"Even a lot of black girls have it easier too. Look at Elba Thomas. She can go out after school, and lately everybody knows she and Eddie Lopez are seeing each other. It's not some big deep secret. I think the Anglo girls got it the best. Remember when I was friendly with Lynne Coleby last year? Her parents are from here, but her grandparents are from someplace in Europe. Anyway, she can go out anytime, anytime at all, just so long as she tells her mother where she is. When I was hanging out with her, Mami didn't like it. Whenever Lynne came over to visit, Mami would start.

"'Why doesn't she telephone first to find out if you are free to play outside?'—or—'Don't her parents care how long she stays visiting you?'—and—'I don't believe in them customs, I'm sorry.'"

"Mami got on my case so bad, I had to stop seeing her. Mami only likes me to hang out with girls who are kept real strict. She loves me to be with Consuela. Although she does like you a lot, but that's because we've been tight for so many years."

"Don't worry, Felita. When you grow up, you can go to art college and do what you want. Your parents won't be able to tell you what to do and your brothers won't boss you. Besides, soon you're going to P.R. to spend the whole summer with your Tio Jorge. No parents or brothers, right?"

"All right!" I felt much better already.

"When are you going over to Vinny's house?" asked Gigi.

"Monday. I hope you're right about what you said." I was feeling so excited at the idea of being Vinny's girl that I could hardly sit still.

"Don't worry, Felita, I'm right. You'll see. . . ."

Response Clue: When reading the details about the narrator's family and friends, students may respond by stating that they are getting to know Felita even better.

Clarification: You may wish to have students stop and reread the introduction to the novel excerpt to understand that Gigi is speaking of Puerto Rico when she uses the term *P.R.*

Additional Skills: This selection is also appropriate for teaching Predicting Outcomes. Remind students that they might find out if their predictions are correct by reading the novel, *Going Home*.

If you are
working on

Lesson 1	Lesson 2
↓	↓
page 2	page 5

from Going Home ■ **11**

Maureen Crane Wartski (1940-   ), born in Japan, often writes about people who come to the United States from southeastern Asia. This story focuses on teenage "boat people" who fled Vietnam in crowded boats. They spent time in refugee camps and often cared for themselves and others without the help of adults until they reached the United States.

from A Long Way from Home

by Maureen Crane Wartski

. . . "Hey, Kien."

Surprised, Kien turned and saw Bob waving to him from across the street. A group of high school students were with him. "Hey, Kien, you're late!" Bob called. "We just finished having our pizza. Want to join us for ice cream?" Kien's stomach growled at the thought of food. He glanced at his watch. It was nearly five o'clock! Had he really been walking around for three hours? No wonder he was hungry!

"I'm coming!" he called and began to walk over to join the others. As he walked, he spotted a stranger in the group, a boy with bright-red hair and broad shoulders. This boy was staring at Kien in an unfriendly way, and, as Kien drew closer, said something to the rest of the group in a derisive tone.

Kien could not hear what this red-haired boy said, but Bob looked surprised. "Kien? He's a good kid!" Bob protested. "Hey, Kien, come meet Sim Evans. He's the new kid I told you about. His dad just got a job here in Bradley."

"Hi," Kien said, but instead of replying, the red-headed boy turned away from Kien and spat on the pavement. He began to walk away. After a few seconds, the others followed. Kien stopped, unsure. Should he go with them or not? He glanced at Bob for guidance. "Bob?" he asked uncertainly.

Bob's cheeks were bright pink. He glanced after the others, then at Kien. "Don't mind Sim," he muttered. "He's new. He doesn't understand."

"Are you coming, Bob?" the redheaded boy called. "You with us, or what?"

Bob looked down at the pavement. "I'll see you at school tomorrow, Kien," he mumbled.

"Okay. Sure . . .," but Bob did not wait to hear what Kien had to say. He was hurrying after Sim Evans and the

others. Kien stood where he was, feeling a little lost. He wished that Bob would turn around and wave, ask him to join them.

"Kien! Where have you been?"

He turned around, staring. Diane, in Steve's car, was waving to him from the curb. What was she doing here? And why was she looking so angry? As Kien ran to the car, Diane cried, "I've been looking all over for you!"

Kien blinked. "You look for . . . me?"

"School let out hours ago!" Diane was very angry. She motioned Kien into the car and added crossly, "When you didn't get home, Mai explained that you were walking. I expected you to be home within the hour. Where have you been?"

Kien couldn't understand why Diane was angry. "Not good I walk?"

Diane stared at him, opened her mouth to speak, then shook her head. "You don't understand, do you? Kien, I was worried." Seeing that he still couldn't understand, she sighed and started the car. "Oh, never mind. Kien, you think so differently from Mai and Loc. Why is that?"

Kien said nothing. The strange, lost feeling that had

Response Clue: Students might note that the narrator is bringing them closer to the feelings of Kien by describing his feelings of being lost and his wish for acceptance.

Response Clue: Even though the outside narrator describes Diane's actions and her tone of voice, the reader does not gain insights into her feelings. Kien is the center of the narrator's focus.

Clarification: You may wish to have students reread the previous paragraph to fully understand why Diane was angry at Kien.

from A Long Way from Home ■ **13**

Response Clue: Again, the narrator is giving the reader insight into Kien's feelings. Students might relate personal experiences in which they too have felt strange, lost, or confused and left out.

Response Clue: The narrator's words give the reader information about Kien's memories of his homeland. Students should recognize that the narrator has complete knowledge of Kien's thoughts and feelings.

Additional Skills: This selection is also appropriate for teaching Making Inferences (see ATE page 21).

Response Clue: Students should recognize that the narrator gives them clues in this paragraph about the reasons for Kien's confusion. Kien is used to independence, even in the face of great danger. He cannot understand why others would worry about him.

begun when Bob turned his back on him was stronger now. He was silent as Diane drove back to the Olsons' home, and when she parked the car he got out without a word and carried his schoolbooks into the house. He could hear Loc and Tad playing someplace, and in the kitchen Mai was on the phone.

"Talking to your friends again," Kien snapped, glad to be able to scold someone. "Women!"

"We're doing our homework," Mai explained, hurt. "Why are you in such a bad temper? And where have you been?"

Kien went into his room and slammed the door. He set his books down on the desk. Homework . . . I should do that too, he thought dismally, but he made no move to open his books. Why? he asked himself. Why can't I be like Mai, like Loc? They are happy here. They like school. Why can't I just settle down?

He sat down at his desk and opened his books and tried to concentrate, but his mind would not stay on his lessons. Instead, his mind filled with images—snow-capped mountains and raging rivers and tall cacti growing in hot, dry deserts. He thought of the oceans, too—oceans where people fished and went to sea in boats. Suddenly, he remembered Phat Dao, the young man he had met on the plane. I wonder if Phat is happy. I wonder how he is doing in Travor.

There was a knock on the door. "Can I come in?" Steve asked, in the doorway. "I'd like to talk to you, Kien."

Steve looked serious as he came to sit on the edge of Kien's bed. Kien felt uncomfortable. "I am in trouble?" he asked, in English.

"Not really. But, Kien, you just can't disappear without telling anyone as you did today. Diane was worried."

"Why, worried?" Kien lapsed into rapid Vietnamese. "Elder Brother, I don't understand. I walked all over Vietnam during the war. I was on a boat that sailed right across the South China Sea. Storms . . . sharks . . . pirates . . . people who didn't want us to land . . . I lived through them all. After our grandfather died on the voyage, I managed to keep Mai and Loc alive. And, in the refugee camp, I worked in the city to buy Mai's medicine." He paused. "Why does Diane worry if I walk in the town?"

Steve looked embarrassed. "You're new here. You could have lost your way."

"If that had happened," Kien said patiently, "I would have gone to a place with a telephone. As you taught me when I first came to America, I would put the smallest silver coin in the slot of the phone, and dial 891-9171. Is that not correct?"

Steve began to laugh. "You are correct, Younger Brother," he said. "I see that there is no reason to worry about your safety. But, Kien," he added in English now, "there are rules."

Kien scowled at the word.

"You see, each of us knows where the others are at all times. That way, no one needs to worry. Next time you go someplace, just tell one of us. That's all!"

Kien nodded slowly. "I tell."

"Good!" Steve reached out to pat Kien's shoulder. "Diane's not angry with you. In fact, she's out there baking a batch of those chocolate-chip brownies you like!"

When Steve had gone, Kien closed his books and stacked them on his desk. He stared past the stack of books toward a window that looked into the backyard. Outside, twilight was turning everything gray, and in that grayness Tad shouted at Loc.

"Loc! Hey, Loc! What'll we play now?"

"Hide-and-seek? How about hide-and-seek?"

"*Tuy ong.* As you like, Loc! I'll be 'it' first. One, two, three . . ."

In the kitchen, Mai laughed. Kien thought, Loc loves it here. Mai is happy here.

"It's not so bad," he said out loud. "I like Mr. Hunter, and Steve is a good man. Diane makes those brownies just for me. And Bob is my friend . . ."

Then he stopped, remembering the big redheaded boy who had spat so contemptuously onto the ground. He remembered the way Bob had gone off with Sim Evans and the others.

Kien drew a long breath and let it out slowly. For the first time in a long while, he felt all alone. . . .

Cultural Awareness: Invite students to discuss members of their own families or friends who came to the United States from other countries. How were their experiences were similar to or different from Kien's?

Additional Skills: This selection is also appropriate for teaching Cultural Context (see ATE page 137).

Response Clue: Here the narrator is describing what Kien sees as he looks out the window. Students might note that it is almost as if the narrator is "inside" Kien's mind. Students might speculate in their notes how they would be responding differently if Kien were telling the story.

Response Clue: Students should use context clues to recognize that *Tuy ong* is a Vietnamese phrase that means "As you like."

Cultural Awareness: You may wish to invite students to do some research on typical foods eaten by people in Vietnam. Encourage students to find out how the typical diet in the United States is different from that in Vietnam.

Additional Skills: Since this selection has been excerpted from a novel, students might like to make some predictions about Kien's adjustments in the United States. Students might like to read the novel and report what happens.

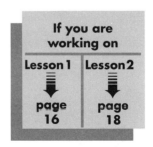

If you are working on

Lesson 1	Lesson 2
⬇	⬇
page 16	page 18

Reviewing the Strategy: Have students refer to the sidenotes they wrote on pages 12-15 to complete the graphic organizer. Have them write answers to the questions on the writing lines.

Lesson 1	Introducing page 2	Practicing page 3	Applying page 4	Reviewing page 16	Testing page 17

Reviewing Point of View

A. Read the excerpt from *A Long Way from Home* on pages 12-15. As you read, write your responses to the point of view in the margins. Use your sidenotes to fill in the diagram.

Question	Look Back	Respond
Who's telling the story? Which words tell me this?	**What are some thoughts and feelings expressed by the main character?** **OR** **What are some story events that are described by an outside narrator?**	**How did the point of view affect my response to the story?**
An outside narrator is telling the story. Words such as *he, his, himself*, and phrases such as *Kien drew closer* tell the reader this.	Accept all appropriate responses that include events described by the outside narrator.	Students should describe their responses to the story as related to the third-person point of view.

Peer Sharing: Have partners read each other's descriptions and compare them. How are they different? How are they the same?

B. Write a brief description of Kien. Write your description in the first person, from Steve's point of view.

Accept all appropriate descriptions written in the first person with the character Steve as the narrator.

Testing **Point of View**

A. The pairs of statements below are based on the excerpt from _A Long Way from Home_ on pages 12-15. Fill in the oval next to the true statement in each pair. On the lines, explain why you chose the statement you did.

● The words _Kien turned and saw Bob waving to him_ tell readers that there is an outside narrator.

○ The words _Kien turned and saw Bob waving to him_ tell readers that Kien is the narrator.

The words _Kien turned_ and _him_ from the story tell readers that there is an outside

narrator who is talking about Kien.

○ The story is written from the first-person point of view.

● The story is written from the third-person point of view.

Because the story is told by an outside narrator who refers to characters as _he_ and

she, the story is told from the third-person point of view.

● In the story, the narrator focuses on the feelings of the main character, Kien.

○ In the story, the narrator tells the feelings of all the characters.

The narrator describes Kien's feelings. The feelings of other characters are not

directly revealed by the narrator.

B. Do you think the story would be better if it were written from a different point of view? On the lines below, give your opinion and then tell why you feel that way.

Accept all appropriate responses. Students should give examples from the novel

excerpt to help support their opinions. They might suggest that they would feel closer

to Kien if it had been written from his point of view.

To begin Lesson 2

page 5

Test-Taking Hints: Tell students they might find it helpful to write sidenotes and organize them on charts as they read test passages. Then they can refer to their notes when answering the test questions.

Meeting Individual Needs: Students who find the skill of point of view challenging may need to go back to the **Introducing** page and review the difference between first-person and third-person point of view.

Clarification: This is called third-person omniscient—where the narrator has inside information about one character.

Reviewing the
Strategy: Have students
identify the phrase from
another language and
fill in the blanks on the
checklist to complete
the graphic organizer.
Students should
identify the language
and write words that
mean about the same as
the phrase and/or words
that are opposite.

Lesson 2	Introducing *page 5*	Practicing *page 6*	Applying *page 7*	Reviewing *page 18*	Testing *page 19*

Reviewing Context Clues

A. Reread the introduction to the story. Then reread page 15 in *A Long Way from Home,* beginning with "When Steve had gone . . ." Notice that the passage contains a phrase from another language. Fill in the checklist below, showing how you used context clues to figure out the meaning of the phrase.

Question	Yes	No	If yes . . .
Are there story clues or author clues that help me identify the other language?	☐	☐	Identify the language. Vietnamese
Can I find a word or words that mean about the same or the opposite of the unfamiliar word?	☐	☐	Write the word or words. As you like.

Peer Sharing: After
students fill in the
checklist, have them
compare their
responses with those of
a peer. What can they
learn from the way that
their partner used
context clues to figure
out the meaning of the
phrase?

B. Why do you think the author chose to include the Vietnamese words *Tuy ong* on page 15 in the story?

Students should recognize that the use of the Vietnamese phrase adds authenticity to

the novel excerpt and gives readers the flavor of another culture.

Oral Language: For
part B, have students
present their position
orally to the group.

Testing Context Clues

A. The following passage contains Vietnamese words in bold type. Read the passage. Read it again and look for clues to the meanings of each foreign word. Then fill in each blank with an English word that gives the meaning of the Vietnamese word.

T'am nodded politely as she sat down at the table. **Bác Chim** was there, enjoying a cup of morning tea. Bác Chim was T'am's ——uncle——, the (brother of her mother.) He
(1)
always had a funny story to tell.

Today, Bác Chim was telling about a time in Vietnam. He had decided to (burn) some brush near his house. His neighbors saw the (blaze) and started shouting, "**Lua chay! Lua chay!** (Fire! Fire!)"

"Why are you yelling '——fire——'?" Bác Chim asked.
(2)
"We thought your house was burning!"

"**Nung lai!** (Stop!)" said Bác Chim. "——Stop—— your
(3)
silliness! Can't you see the old **hai** I'm (wearing on my feet?) If my house were burning, I'd be sure to save my new

——shoes—— for work!"
(4)

B. At the end of the excerpt from *A Long Way from Home*, Kien felt all alone. Why do you think he felt that way? Use examples from the story to support your response.

Accept all appropriate responses. Students should consider the fact that Kien was in a

new country and was confused about the appropriate way to act. In addition, he had

experienced rejection from boys at his school.

Test-Taking Hints: Point out that the Vietnamese words are in dark print. Remind students to read the passage completely at least once before filling in the blanks with English words.

ESL/LEP: Students might like to create their own cloze passages using words from their first languages. Remind students to provide some clues to the meaning of the non-English words. Use words in this lesson to begin a classroom dictionary of words from other languages.

Meeting Individual Needs: Help students circle context clues.

Writing Self-Assessment: Students might wish to evaluate their own writing on a scale of 1-4, with 1 being the least degree and 4 being the greatest degree. Have them use the following criteria: Did I have a topic sentence? Did I answer the question? Are my ideas stated clearly? Did I use examples from the selection?

Unit TWO

BECOMING AN ACTIVE READER

When reading **novel excerpts**, good readers pay attention to an author's choice of words. Good readers use these words to help them visualize what is happening.

Using Skills and Strategies

Inferring the setting will help you create mental pictures as you read. You might ask: Where does the story take place? How is it similar to a place I know? When does the story take place? What do I know about this time? How does the setting affect the plot of the story?

Noting the **sensory words** is another way to imagine what is happening. You might ask: How do these words help me imagine the story? Do they appeal to my sense of touch, sight, sound, smell, or taste?

In this unit, **making inferences** about the setting and identifying **sensory words** will help you read the stories more actively.

Reading The Novel Excerpt

You know a good story when you read one. But what is it about a good story that makes the action come alive? Often, the writer's own background and experiences written into the plot make a story memorable. As you read the excerpts in this unit, keep in mind the cultural perspectives from which the authors have written their stories.

Responding to Novel Excerpts

Good readers often imagine that they are a part of the story. By picturing the setting, they see themselves right there—watching the story firsthand. Remember to jot down your thoughts about the setting while reading the excerpts from *Journey Home* and *Let the Circle Be Unbroken*. Writing these sidenotes will help you remember how the setting helps you to experience the story. Use your notes as you discuss the excerpts with your classmates.

Unit Enrichment: Have the novels *Journey Home* and *Let the Circle Be Unbroken* available in the classroom for students to read. Or, read aloud from one of them each day. Discuss with students the part the excerpts play in the novels.

Meeting Individual Needs: For extra credit, students might like to do research and report to the class on the events in U.S. history that served as the background for each novel.

Making Inferences

| *Lesson 3* | **Introducing**
 page 21 | **Practicing**
 page 22 | **Applying**
 page 23 | **Reviewing**
 page 32 | **Testing**
 page 33 |

Introducing Strategies

Reading is like putting together puzzle pieces. Good readers are always connecting words and ideas to see the whole picture. Sometimes, authors do not include all the necessary words and ideas. Then, readers must **make inferences.** Making inferences is like finding the missing puzzle pieces. Readers do this by relating story details to their own experiences.

The puzzle pieces below show how readers make inferences about story **setting.** First, readers find details about time and place. Next, they relate those clues to what they already know. Then, they come up with the missing information, or inference.

Story Clues About Time and Place + What the Reader Already Knows = Inferences About the Setting

Reading the Novel Excerpt

Read the excerpt from the novel *Journey Home* on pages 27-28 and the sample sidenotes on page 27. These notes show how one good reader made inferences about the story's setting. After reading, complete the items below.

1. List details from the first three paragraphs that may have helped the reader infer that the story opens in a dream or in an unreal place.

"screaming wind, fine sand choking her" "I can't see... breathe... " "vanishing

world... eerie... stumbled, gagging"

2. What in the reader's experience might have led him or her to infer that the opening is a dream?

Accept any appropriate responses showing that the student used personal experience

to infer the setting.

Lesson Objective: To make inferences about the setting in excerpts from *Journey Home* and *Let the Circle Be Unbroken* by noting details and relating them to personal experiences.

Oral Language: Discuss with students how they make inferences every day. Have them describe the classroom setting without specifically saying it's a classroom or a school. Remind them that the setting includes time and place.

Modeling the Strategy: Read aloud an appropriate passage from your own reading and model how you make inferences about the setting. Refer to the steps in the diagram. Use the Reproducible Activity Master on page T11 of the ATE to help students apply the strategy to the excerpt from *Journey Home.*

Managing the Lesson: Remind students to carefully read the sidenotes on page 27 as they read the selection and use them to answer these questions. Point out that the notes model the process of inferring the setting described in the graphic organizer.

Practicing *Making Inferences*

A. The incomplete sentences below are about the excerpt from *Journey Home*. Circle the letter in front of the choice that best completes each sentence. Then, on the lines provided, write details from the story that helped you make that choice.

1. Yuki's dream takes place
   a. during a snowstorm.
   (b.) during a sandstorm.
   c. at a sandy beach.
   d. in Salt Lake City.

Students may mention "desert wind," "swirling dust," "sand so fine" it blinded
and choked her.

2. Yuki and her family left the camp at Topaz because
   a. they had been there a year.
   b. the camp director told them to go.
   (c.) agitators might have harmed them.
   d. they had wanted to stay.

Students may mention threats from camp agitators and the stink bomb thrown into
the family's barrack room.

3. When she woke up, seeing familiar things in her room helped Yuki feel
   (a.) relieved.   c. grateful.
   b. threatened.   d. shaky.

Students may suggest that Yuki felt shaky until she had identified the chest of
drawers, the armchair, the picture.

B. Describe a dream. In your description, give clues to help readers infer the setting of the dream.

Accept all appropriate responses. Students may need some direction in providing

details that will help the reader infer the setting.

_____

_____

_____

_____

_____

Purpose: The purpose of the **Practicing** page is to help students practice using details and prior knowledge to infer setting. The questions reflect the puzzle strategy illustrated on the **Introducing** page.

Peer Sharing: Have students complete Section A with a classmate. Both partners should be able to explain why they made the choices they did.

Assessing Student Writing: Rate student writing on a scale of 1-4, with 1 being the least degree and 4 being the greatest degree. Use the following criteria: originality, organization, reasoning, and clarity.

Applying **Making Inferences**

A. Read the following paragraph. Combine the clues given by the writer with your own experiences to make inferences about the setting. Then complete the items below.

> *Jorge was tired and had a headache. He had worked hard all night at the store downstairs and wanted to sleep now. With the shade pulled, the room was almost dark. He rested on the couch, listening to sounds from outside. He heard a motorcycle in the steady stream of traffic on the street. There was the whoosh of the bus door opening, closing. These were familiar sounds. Even the roar of the subway train was comforting, and Jorge smiled as he drifted off to sleep.*

1. List at least five words or phrases that are clues to the setting.

Accept all appropriate responses that suggest an urban, daytime setting: worked all

night, room almost dark with the shade pulled, traffic sounds, store downstairs.

2. What do you already know that helped you make inferences about the setting?

Accept all appropriate responses that support their inferences about the setting.

3. What inferences did you make about where and when this story takes place?

Appropriate responses would include: apartment over a store on a busy street in a

city; modern time; in the morning.

B. Write a brief paragraph describing what you think might happen next to Jorge. In your description, give more clues about the setting.

Responses should include appropriate details about the urban setting.

Applying the Skill to Other Media: Remind students that they might need to infer the setting of an unfamiliar TV program or movie. Discuss with them what clues they might use. Students might suggest clothing, hairstyles, types of transportation, types of homes, or dialects.

Individualized Learning: Have students complete Section A independently. Make sure they use specific details mentioned in the paragraph and their own experiences to complete items 1 and 2.

Conferencing: After writing, have students exchange papers to check the clarity of each other's clues. Students may wish to ask: How might the clues to the setting have been stated more clearly? Is the setting in the paragraphs consistent with the setting in the passage?

To review ↓ page 32

Sensory Language

Lesson Objective: To identify and respond to sensory language in the excerpts from *Journey Home* and *Let the Circle Be Unbroken*.

ESL/LEP: Make available or have students find pictures of familiar items that evoke a sensory response for example, foods, street scenes, or flowers. Ask students to describe the image by telling what they see (colors), hear (sounds), taste (consistency), feel (textures), smell (sweet).

Modeling the Strategy:
Read aloud a sentence from a passage that contains an example of sensory words. (Advertisements in magazines might be a good source). Refer to the categories on the chart as you read. After completing this page, have students copy the diagram on page 34 in their notebooks and use it to apply the strategy to the excerpt from *Journey Home*.

Introducing Strategies

Authors want their stories to make lasting impressions on their readers. One way they do this is to use **sensory** words. Sensory words and phrases appeal to a reader's sense of sound, sight, touch, smell, and taste. Good readers respond to sensory words by imagining what they "hear," "see," "taste," "smell," or "touch." Imagining through the senses what the author is describing helps the story make a lasting impression on the reader.

The chart below shows how readers respond to sensory words.

Sensory Words From the Story	RESPONSES				
	What do I "see"?	What do I "hear"?	What do I "feel"?	What do I "taste"?	What do I "smell"?
		(Words that tell what I imagine)			

Reading the Novel Excerpt

Reread the excerpt from *Journey Home* on pages 27-28. As you read, underline examples of sensory language. Think about how these words helped you respond to the story through your senses. Then complete the two items below.

1. List some of the sensory words and phrases you underlined as you read.

Students may mention such phrases as "screaming desert wind," "stifling her,"

"smothering," "choking dust," "sting of sand," "pounding heart," "toilet filled with filth."

2. Tell how you responded to each example you listed above. Refer to the headings on the chart to guide you as you write your answers.

Students may imagine hearing high-pitched sounds or tasting a dry, gritty,

chalk-like substance.

Practicing *Sensory Language*

A. Circle the letter in front of the choice that best completes each sentence below. Then, on the lines provided, tell why you made the choice you did.

1. The words *white powdery sand in her face* may cause the reader to imagine feeling

    a. cold.   c. squishy and soft.

    (b.) dry and gritty.   d. nervous.

Students may mention sand is dry and gritty.

_____

2. The words *screaming desert wind* may cause the reader to hear

    a. a dull thud.   c. gentle laughter.

    (b.) shrieking sounds.   d. both b and c.

Students may suggest that a screaming wind is neither dull nor gentle.

_____

3. A reader might respond to the words *all alone in an eerie unreal world* by seeing

    a. crowds of people.   c. white, puffy clouds.

    b. the wind blowing.   (d.) a dark, empty space.

Students may mention that a dark empty space would seem eerie if it

were unfamiliar.

B. Imagine you are writing a scene for a movie or play. Describe a frightening experience. Use sensory words so that the incident will appeal to the viewer's sense of sight, sound, touch, taste, and smell.

Accept all appropriate responses. Note that students could write about an incident

that happened to someone else or describe something seen on TV or in a movie.

_____

_____

_____

_____

_____

_____

Purpose: The purpose of the **Practicing** page is to help students use their imaginations to respond to sensory words in the novel excerpt.

Peer Sharing: Have students complete Section A independently, then work with a partner to compare answers. Encourage students to make sure their partners provide adequate evidence from their own experiences to support their responses.

Cooperative Learning: Suggest that students work in small groups to write about a frightening experience that they could develop for a Readers' Theatre performance.

Applying *Sensory Language*

Applying the Skill to Other Media: Suggest that students pay attention to the sensory words in the lyrics when they listen to popular music.

Cooperative Learning: Have students complete Section A in groups of three, with one student the reader, another the moderator, the third the recorder. Tell students there need not be consensus on their responses, but each response should be supported with evidence.

A. The following description is an excerpt from Nicholasa Mohr's novel *Going Home*. The narrator, a Puerto Rican girl from New York City, is visiting Puerto Rico for the first time. Read the excerpt. Then complete the page.

> *. . . I had to admit that, even if there wasn't much to do here, it sure was pretty. From where I sat I could see the surrounding mountains and all the houses, mules, horses, and square patches of earth where different vegetables were growing. Fruit trees stood next to tall palm trees that swayed in the breeze. The narrow country roads had cars and trucks going back and forth on them. . . . I took a deep breath, inhaling the sweet and spicy smells of the flowers and vegetables all mixed up together. It felt really good to breathe this air. . . .*

1. List four examples of sensory words in the passage.

Accept reasonable responses. Students may mention "square patches of earth," "fruit

trees next to palm trees," "palm trees swayed," "sweet and spicy smells."

2. How did you respond as you read each phrase listed above? Describe what you "saw," "heard," "smelled," "tasted," or "touched."

Accept reasonable responses that relate student experiences with the items listed.

Writing Process: Students might choose to develop their descriptions into the first drafts of a poem.

B. Write a paragraph that describes a place that is very different from where you live. Use sensory words to help your reader "smell," "taste," "feel," "hear," and "see" what you are describing.

Accept appropriate responses. Encourage students to supply details that help readers

imagine the place through their senses.

To review

⬇

page 34

Yoshiko Uchida (1921-1992) wrote many books for young people that dealt with her Japanese ancestry and with Japanese American history. During World War II, Americans of Japanese descent living on the west coast of the United States were ordered from their homes and moved to camps like the one described in the excerpt below. Uchida and her family were among these people.

Preteaching Vocabulary: You may wish to preteach the following words: *barrack, chintz.*

Accessing Prior Knowledge: Have available some background information on the internment of 110,000 Japanese Americans during World War II. Have students brainstorm what it might be like to have to pick up and move into a barracks-type of living situation.

from Journey Home

by Yoshiko Uchida

. . . I can't see, Yuki thought frantically. I can't breathe.

The screaming desert wind flung its white powdery sand in her face, stifling her and wrapping her up in a smothering cocoon of sand so fine it was like dust. It blinded her and choked her and made her gag as she opened her mouth to cry out.

The black tar-papered barracks on either side of the road had vanished behind the swirling dust, and Yuki was all alone in an eerie, unreal world where nothing existed except the shrieking wind and the great choking clouds of dust. Yuki stumbled on, doubled over, pushing hard against the wind, gasping as she felt the sting of sand and pebbles against her legs.

Suppose she never got back to her barrack? Suppose the wind simply picked her up and flung her out beyond the barbed wire fence into the desert? Suppose no one ever found her dried, wind-blown body out there in the sagebrush?

A cry of terror swelled up inside her. "Mama! Papa! Help me!"

The sound of her own scream woke her up. Yuki's heart was pounding. Her damp fists were clenched tight. Her face was wet with tears.

For several minutes she couldn't believe it was only a nightmare. It had all seemed so real, she could almost taste the flat, powdery dust in her mouth. She had been back in the Utah desert, living with Mama and Papa and her big brother, Ken, in Topaz, one of the World War II concentration camps where all the Japanese of the West Coast had been sent by the government.

Yuki shuddered and blinked hard, trying to see where she really was. Was she back in the small crowded

The sidenotes on this page show how one reader made inferences about the setting of the story.

◀ She can't see or breathe. Where is she? Is this real?

Response Clue: Underlining reflects sensory language students may have identified.

◀ She talks about things vanishing; an eerie, unreal world; and the "shrieking wind." It seems to me that this story opens with a nightmare. I've had some weird, scary dreams myself.

◀ She sees barracks and a barbed wire fence. Could she be in prison?

◀ It was a bad dream—probably about being in the barracks—but where is she now?

Response Clue: Students should identify clues that show the shift in story setting from unreal to real.

Meeting Individual Needs:
Encourage students to continue writing notes about the setting—where Yuki is and the place that she is remembering.

Response Clue: Students may recall their own experiences of the difficulty in separating a dream and the "real" world when waking up.

ESL/LEP: Have students share their experiences moving here from another country or from a very different place (moving, for instance, to a city from a rural environment).

Clarification: You may wish to have students reread this paragraph to clarify that Yuki is remembering something in the past; this is not part of the dream nor the actual present.

Response Clue: Students' notes might reflect on how Yuki's two real worlds differ.

barrack room where their four army cots were separated by army blankets strung on ropes? Would she have to wake Mama and ask her to bring the flashlight and go out to the latrine with her because she was too scared to go alone? Would she have to rush from toilet to toilet to find one that wasn't filled with filth because the water had stopped running?

Yuki gathered herself up into a small ball and hugged her knees. Gradually, slowly, she left the strange world of dreams and nightmares and knew she was safe in her room in the apartment in Salt Lake City, which the minister of the Japanese church had found for them. And he'd told them not to worry because the landlady, Mrs. Henley, didn't mind their being Japanese.

For a few moments Yuki remembered again the awful fear that had consumed her those last weeks in Topaz when Papa had been threatened by the small gang of agitators. They had turned their anger at being in camp against anyone who, like Papa, worked with the administration to keep the camp running smoothly. And finally, one night, they had thrown a stink bomb into their barrack room. After that both Mama and Papa knew it was no longer safe to remain in camp, even though they wanted to stay and do whatever they could to help their people.

"Your family has already spent almost a year in camp," the director had said to Papa. "I think it's time now that you left."

He had secured special clearance for them to leave, and they had gone to Salt Lake City as soon as possible. Now they were safe outside the camp, and there was no more barbed wire fence to keep them from going anywhere they wanted to go.

Yuki took a deep breath and wiped her nose with the corner of the sheet. Mama wouldn't like her doing that, but she was still too shaky to get out of bed. She stared into the darkness until she could make out the familiar things in her room: the big, carved-oak chest of drawers that Mrs. Henley's great-grandfather had built, the small, chintz-covered armchair that was Yuki's favorite chair in the whole apartment, and the large gold frame on the wall with the watercolor scene of sailboats in a sunny harbor.

Yes, everything was all there. It was all right. She was safe, and she needn't ever worry again about being blown into the desert to turn into a heap of sun-bleached bones....

If you are working on

Lesson 3	Lesson 4
↓	↓
page 21	page 24

Mildred Taylor (1943-) says she wrote this novel to honor past generations in her family. Cassie, the main character, watches her elders denied their right to vote even though African Americans had by law been given this right nearly 100 years before. According to Taylor, the reactions of children like Cassie to the courage of the adults around her led to the civil rights movement of the 1950s and 1960s.

from Let the Circle Be Unbroken

by Mildred Taylor

. . . "I thinks I wants to vote," announced Mrs. Lee Annie one <u>rainy afternoon in mid-April</u> as she sat with Big Ma and me <u>in front of the fire finishing a patchwork</u> quilt started in winter.

Big Ma looked <u>sharply</u> across at her old friend. "Say what?"

"You heard me. Said I was gon' vote."

Big Ma's fingers moved deftly over the patch that had once been a part of Little Man's trousers to make sure it hadn't <u>puckered</u>. "Lord-a-mercy, Lee Annie, you gone foolish in yo' old age?"

"Naw . . . I just wants to vote. Done made up my mind."

"But Miz Lee Annie, you said you didn't wanna vote," I reminded her as I took this opportunity to put aside the quilting which had been forced upon me by Big Ma as one of those things young ladies needed to learn. "You said you just wanted to read that constitution."

"Well, that's the truth all right, sugar. But I jus' been thinking. Now's I'm learning the law, why shouldn't I jus' go on down and vote jus' like them white folks—"

"You done gone foolish—" Big Ma said again.

"Probably knows it better than a lot of them," Mrs. Lee Annie continued, unperturbed. "My papa voted. Said it was a right fine feeling. He voted and he didn't know no law at all 'ceptin' that he was a free man and a free man could vote. And here I jus' been readin' the constitution, and I ain't votin' at all—"

"You been readin' too much, that's what you been doin'," Big Ma retorted.

"Well, I'm gon' do it, Caroline. Gon' vote . . . sho' is. Where that Mary? Ow, you, Mary! Where you at?"

Preteaching Vocabulary: You may wish to preteach the following vocabulary: *civil rights movement, puckered, registrar, radiant.*

Accessing Prior Knowledge: Have students read the title and the headnote. Have students share with a partner what they know about the civil rights movement.

As you read, make inferences about the setting of the story. Use the margins to note story details and what you already know that help you to infer the setting.

Response Clue: Students may have underlined clues to time and place, such as "rainy afternoon," "mid-April," and "in front of the fire." Discuss how students could infer the setting from the first sentence in the selection.

ESL/LEP: If you have students from several different countries in your class, ask them to share their native countries' voting practices. Is there a word for "vote" in their native language? Suggest that students interview a relative, if necessary.

Response Clue: If students have difficulty understanding the dialect, read the dialogue aloud and discuss what the words mean. Students might use the Southern dialect as a clue to the rural South setting.

Prior Knowledge: Remind students that although African American *men* could vote after the Emancipation Proclamation in 1863, no woman could vote until 1920 with the passage of the 19th Amendment to the Constitution.

Response Clue: Students'
notes might reflect what it
would be like not being
represented, not being
allowed to do something that
is your right by law.
Students may have inferred
the setting from "She free
and she gon' vote."

Response Clue: Poll taxes
are an important clue to the
rural South setting. Mention
to students, however, that
since such taxes existed in
southern states even into the
1950s, this story could have
taken place up until that time
or into the 1960s.

Making Predictions: Ask
students what they think
Mrs. Lee Annie will do since
her family and friends do not
agree with her.

Additional Skills: This
selection is also appropriate
for teaching Context Clues to
understand slang (see ATE
page 137).

Mama came in from the kitchen and Mrs. Lee Annie told her what she had told us. Mama glanced from Mrs. Lee Annie to Big Ma.

"Don't look at me," Big Ma said. "I done told her she was crazy. 'Round here talkin' 'bout she free and she gon' vote . . . like she got somebody to vote for."

Mama came back to the circle and took her seat, but she didn't pick up the quilt. Instead, she put her hand on Mrs. Lee Annie's arm. "Now, Mrs. Lee Annie," she said, "why you want to do this thing? You know these people aren't going to let you vote."

"I knows what I gotta do to take that test," Mrs. Lee Annie contended stubbornly, pounding her knee through the heavy quilt for emphasis. "I gots to have my poll taxes paid—and they gonna be, Russell give me the money—and I gotta tell the registrar what them there words in the constitution mean—and I gonna be able to do that—then I can vote."

"Mrs. Lee Annie, how many colored folks you know vote?"

"Ne'er a one. But part of that's 'cause these ole white folks think ain't no colored folks gon' come down to their ole voting places to vote. Well, this here ole aunty gon' strut right down there and show them I knows the law. Ole Lee Annie Lees gon' vote jus' like her daddy done."

"Now, Mrs. Lee Annie—"

"Lee Annie Lees, that's 'bout the silliest thing I done heard of!" exclaimed Big Ma in exasperation. "Now jus' who you think you gon' vote for if they lets you vote? Bilbo?"

"Humph!" grumped Mrs. Lee Annie.

"Mrs. Lee Annie," Mama said, "now have you thought about what could happen if you try to register? First of all, they most likely won't even let you, and even if they do, they won't pass you on the test, but they'll remember you tried to vote and they won't think too kindly of you for it either."

"That ain't what I'm living for, for these crackers to think kindly of me!"

Mama smiled and nodded. "But more than that, have you thought of what Harlan Granger might say?"

Mrs. Lee Annie looked surprised. "Harlan Granger? What he got to do with it?"

Mama took Mrs. Lee Annie's hand. "You're living on his land and he expects certain things—"

"And I gives 'em to him, too! Works my land and puts in my crop 'longside Page and Leora every year."

"Yes, ma'am, I know that, but—"

"And he knows it too!"

"Yes, ma'am. But Harlan Granger doesn't expect you to go off trying to vote, and he's not going to like it. Not one little bit."

For the first time Mrs. Lee Annie was silent.

"He's not going to care," Mama continued, "about your papa or your dreams. All he's going to care about is that one of 'his' colored people is trying to do something he figures is white folks' business, and believe me, Mrs. Lee Annie—I know that man—when he doesn't like something, that means there's going to be trouble . . . for you. . . . Things could happen."

Mrs. Lee Annie was thoughtful, one hand fingering the quilt, the other still held by Mama. She remained unspeaking for so long that Mama finally said, "Mrs. Lee Annie?"

Mrs. Lee Annie looked back at Mama. "Mary, child, all my life whenever I wanted to do something and the white folks didn't like it, I didn't do it. All my life, it been that way. But now I's sixty-four years old and I figure I's deserving of doing something I wants to do, white folks like it or not. And this old body wants to vote and like I done said, I gots my mind made up. I's gon' vote too."

Mama patted her hand. "Promise me you'll think about what I said."

"I'll think 'bout it all right, but it ain't gonna change my mind none. What I really want though is for you to help me. You and Cassie. What Cassie and me ain't learned, you can teach us. Will you do that for me, sugar?"

"Mrs. Lee Annie—"

"I said I'd think 'bout it, ain't I? But I still wants your help."

Mama puckered her lips and sighed. "You think about what I said and you think hard now—"

"And you gonna help me?"

"It's against my better judgment . . ."

"But ya will?"

Mama shook her head, allowing a frustrated laugh. "I suppose."

"Good!" said Mrs. Lee Annie, smiling <u>brightly</u> and picking up her quilting. . . .

Making Predictions: Ask students to stop reading at this point and predict what they think might happen. Suggest students read the novel to find out if their predictions were correct.

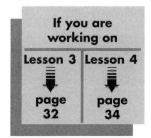

If you are working on

Lesson 3 | Lesson 4

page 32 | page 34

Reviewing the Strategy: To complete the graphic organizer, have students refer to the sidenotes they wrote on pages 29-31 in which they identified details that helped them infer the setting. Remind them to use the clues given in the excerpt as well as information they already know.

Reviewing *Making Inferences*

A. Read the excerpt from *Let the Circle Be Unbroken* on pages 29-31. Reread the introduction on page 29. Make some inferences about the setting in the margins. Then use your notes to fill in the puzzle pieces.

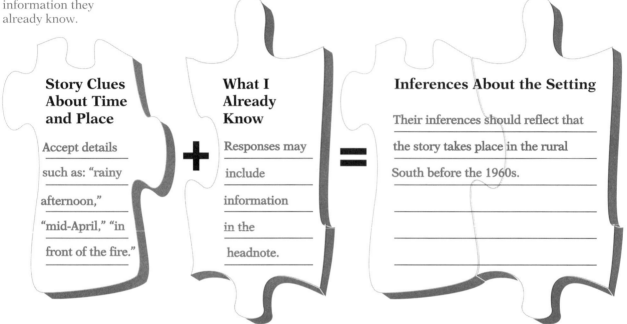

Story Clues About Time and Place

Accept details such as: "rainy afternoon," "mid-April," "in front of the fire."

+

What I Already Know

Responses may include information in the headnote.

=

Inferences About the Setting

Their inferences should reflect that the story takes place in the rural South before the 1960s.

Meeting Individual Needs: Caution students not to confuse influences of setting (time and place) with those of other characters (motivations of other people).

Managing the Lesson: Answers in the puzzle are suggestions. Students may find other details that give clues to the setting such as poll taxes, which were levied in the South.

B. Write a paragraph. Think about an injustice you have read or heard about. Write a paragraph that describes how the time and place of the incident may have influenced what happened.

Paragraphs should include student's own feelings and ideas as they make inferences

about the setting. These details should contribute to an understanding of the incident.

_____

_____

_____

_____

_____

_____

_____

_____

_____

_____

Testing *Making Inferences*

Test-Taking Hints: Remind students that they need to decide on the *best* response of those given. Suggest that if students have trouble with one question they should continue with the other questions in the section and then go back and rethink the problem.

A. These items are about the excerpt from *Let the Circle Be Unbroken*, pages 29-31. Read each question and the choices that follow. Fill in the circle in front of the choice that best answers the question.

1. Why does Mrs. Lee Annie's plan to vote alarm the others?
   ○ a. The African American slaves have not been freed.
   ● b. African Americans in the South were often kept from voting.
   ○ c. Women were not allowed to vote.
   ○ d. Mrs. Lee Annie does not live in the United States.

2. How does Mrs. Lee Annie feel about having always done what the white folks wanted?
   ○ a. pleased
   ○ b. proud
   ● c. resentful
   ○ d. satisfied

3. Why is voting so important to Mrs. Lee Annie?
   ● a. It is her right.
   ○ b. All African Americans voted.
   ○ c. She became interested in the law.
   ○ d. She paid her poll tax.

4. Why does Cassie's mama say it is "against my better judgment" to help Mrs. Lee Annie?
   ○ a. She thought Mrs. Lee Annie couldn't learn.
   ○ b. She didn't think she was smart enough to teach.
   ● c. She thought Mrs. Lee Annie was heading for trouble and didn't want to encourage her.
   ○ d. She doesn't know Harlan Granger at all.

B. Write a paragraph to explain the effects of the setting on Mrs. Lee Annie.

Accept all reasonable responses. Students might suggest that in another setting—

outside the South, for instance—Mrs. Lee Annie would have always voted, or there

wouldn't be a question of her being allowed to do so.

To begin
Lesson 4

↓

page
24

Lesson 4	Introducing *page 24*	Practicing *page 25*	Applying *page 26*	Reviewing *page 34*	Testing *page 35*

Reviewing the Strategy: Remind students that sensory words help readers experience the story as if they were there. To complete the graphic organizer, they will need to refer to the words they underlined at the beginning of the selection.

Managing the Lesson: Answers on the chart are suggestions. Students may find additional sensory words such as *strut, puckered, brightly.*

Reviewing Sensory Language

A. Reread the excerpt from *Let the Circle Be Unbroken* on pages 29-31. In the excerpt, Taylor has used sensory words to create a warm, friendly atmosphere inside the house.

- **Underline the words at the beginning of the excerpt that helped you create this picture in your mind.**
- **Write the words in the chart below and fill in your responses.**
- **Then add some of your own sensory words to the chart that might help to create an even stronger image of the same scene.**

Sensory Words From the Story	RESPONSES				
	What do I "see"?	What do I "hear"?	What do I "feel"?	What do I "taste"?	What do I "smell"?
fire		crackling	warmth		
sharply	a wrinkled brow				
pounding			aching		

Assessing Student Writing: Rate student writing on a scale of 1-4, with 1 being the least degree and 4 being the greatest degree. Use the following criteria: uses topic sentences, uses supporting details from the text, develops ideas logically, and uses closing sentence.

B. Write a paragraph that compares the warm, caring atmosphere inside the house with the cold, unjust world outside. In your paragraph, explain how the author's use of sensory language at the beginning of the story helped create that atmosphere.

Accept reasonable responses. Students may mention that the people inside cared about each other and what they thought while the outside world didn't [by not caring about their vote].

Testing Sensory Language

A. Read the passage below. Read it a second time and fill each blank with a word from the word pairs listed in the right-hand margin. Choose the word that best appeals to your sense of sight, sound, touch, taste or smell.

The _____piercing_____ cold wind _____whistled_____ and
        (1)   **(2)**

howled through the _____deep_____, dark woods. The snow
                 (3)

was so _____thick_____ that it shut out the light of day. Flakes
        (4)

that looked like open _____parachutes_____ built soft white
               (5)

mounds on unprotected branches. The terrified child with a

_____hollow_____, pale face stood _____shivering_____ at the
  (6)   **(7)**

doorway of the _____cottage_____, the _____bitter_____ cold
           (8)   **(9)**

penetrating her _____drab_____ brown coat. _____jagged_____
         (10)   **(11)**

icicles hung above the doorway like great _____teeth_____.
                                (12)

B. Write a paragraph describing a scene from a movie that made an impression on you. Use words that will appeal to the reader's sense of sight, sound, touch, taste, and smell.

Suggest that students select a movie that has a lot of action or unusual scenery.

_____

_____

_____

_____

_____

_____

_____

_____

_____

_____

_____

Meeting Individual Needs: Allow some latitude in the answers, particularly items 3, 7, 8, 9, 10, 11. Students may imagine the scene differently.

1. powdery
   piercing
2. blew
   whistled
3. deep
   big
4. cold
   thick
5. parachutes
   boxes
6. hollow
   radiant
7. still
   shivering
8. house
   cottage
9. bitter
   winter
10. drab
    dark
11. Jagged
    Long
12. spokes
    teeth

Peer Sharing: After completing their paragraphs, have students exchange papers with a classmate. Tell students to respond to the sensory language in their partner's paragraph by making at least two positive comments.

Unit *THREE*

BECOMING AN ACTIVE READER

Active readers are critical readers. They pay careful attention to the information in **newspaper articles** they read. They form opinions and ask questions. Good readers also look for connections between what they read and what they already know.

Using Skills and Strategies

Making **comparisons and contrasts** will help you gather information from newspaper articles that you read. You might ask: How is this similar to something the author said earlier or to what I read in another article? In what ways is it different? What do I already know about this subject?

Identifying **key words** also helps you to read articles critically. You might ask: Which words name important ideas? How are these words related to the subject?

In this unit, **comparing and contrasting** and identifying **key words** will help you to read critically.

Reading Newspaper Articles

People read newspaper articles to stay up to date. They want to know about the lives of people who work in unique jobs and participate in popular activities. A newspaper's sports section and business section contain articles of timely interest to their readers. Readers of newspaper articles not only want to be entertained but also want to stay informed.

Responding to Newspaper Articles

It is important to jot down questions and responses as you read the two articles in this unit, "Laura Weber: One Native American Whose Business Is the Environment" and "The Alomars—Baseball's Version of *All in the Family.*" Refer to your notes as you discuss the articles with your classmates.

Unit Enrichment:
Have students work in groups to analyze waste management practices in their school. Encourage them to interview teachers and custodial staff about their needs. Then ask them to write an environmental report card that includes suggestions about managing school waste better.

Compare and Contrast

Lesson 5	Introducing page 37	Practicing page 38	Applying page 39	Reviewing page 52	Testing page 53

Introducing Strategies

Good readers make connections among people, facts, and ideas as they read articles. One way they make these connections is to **compare** and **contrast** information. Comparing is noticing the ways events, people, and ideas are alike. Contrasting is noticing how they are different. Good readers also ask themselves questions such as: How are the people alike? How are they different? In what ways are these events similar to each other? How are they different? You may think of some questions of your own to ask.

The diagram below shows one way readers organize their thinking as they compare and contrast information.

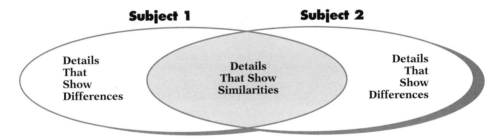

Reading the Newspaper Article

Read the newspaper article about Laura Weber on pages 43-46 and the sidenotes on pages 43-44. These notes show how one good reader contrasted Weber's early life with her later life. After reading, answer these questions.

1. What did the reader note about how Weber's early life was different from her college and adult years?

Accept all appropriate responses. For example, Weber received poor high school

grades, but she earned college degrees and started her own company; she hated

science but majored in it; her involvement with Native American heritage changed.

2. According to the reader, what things remained the same?

Her determination to work hard and get an education and her respect for her Native

American heritage.

Lesson Objective: To compare and contrast information in the articles "Laura Weber: One Native American Whose Business Is the Environment" and "The Alomars—Baseball's Version of *All in the Family*" by using a Venn diagram.

ESL/LEP: Have available two similar objects, such as two kinds of fruit, an apple and a ball, or a desk and a table. Ask students to identify their similarities and differences.

Modeling the Strategy: Read aloud a passage from students' classroom texts to model comparing and contrasting. Show students how the Venn diagram can be used to group similarities and differences. Use the Reproducible Activity Master on page T13 of the ATE to help students apply the Venn diagram strategy to the article about Laura Weber.

Managing the Lesson: Remind students to use the sidenotes on pages 43-44 to complete this page. The sidenotes model the process of active reading, by comparing and contrasting information.

Lesson 5	Introducing *page 37*	Practicing *page 38*	Applying *page 39*	Reviewing *page 52*	Testing *page 53*

Practicing *Compare and Contrast*

Purpose: The purpose of the **Practicing** page is to help students practice the skill of comparing and contrasting information in a nonfiction article. Questions reflect the Venn diagram strategy on the **Introducing** page.

Peer Sharing: Have students complete Section A with a classmate. Partners should both be able to explain the choices they made.

A. The incomplete statements below are based on the newspaper article about Laura Weber. Circle the letter in front of the phrase that best completes each statement. Then, on the lines provided, explain why you made the choice you did.

1. In comparing her early life with her later life, Laura Weber probably never imagined
   a. she was a Mohawk.
   b. she would have a career in science.
   c. she would paint bridges.
   d. none of the above.
   She disliked science before she went to college.

2. Laura Weber's interest in her Native American Heritage
   a. increased as she became associated with AISES.
   b. increased when she entered college.
   c. has remained the same throughout her life.
   d. all of the above.
   After attending an AISES conferences, she felt more connected with her heritage.

3. One thing that has remained constant in Laura Weber's life is
   a. her belief in herself.
   b. her pride in being a Mohawk.
   c. her ability to get good grades.
   d. her interest in chemistry.
   She was determined to go to college and to help the environment.

Writing Process: Students might begin a personal journal, noting ways they have changed or have stayed the same as they have matured.

B. Think about a hobby or activity that you were once interested in. Compare and contrast it to one that interests you now. Explain how the two are alike and how they are different.

Accept all appropriate responses. Students should provide details to illustrate the

comparisons they make.

_____

_____

_____

_____

Applying *Compare and Contrast*

Read the following paragraph. Think about how the writer is comparing two things. Then answer the questions that follow.

> *The earliest schools were founded in 3500 B.C. in Sumer, an ancient country that is now part of Iraq. In some ways, these early schools were like schools today. Students did homework, recited lessons, and had tests, just as you do, in literature, mathematics, and art. But Sumerian schools were also very different from schools today. Only boys could attend school in Sumer. Students learned to write by copying the same literary selection over and over again, and they learned mathematics by copying business accounts over and over again. Sumerian students wrote their lessons by scratching characters into a damp clay tablet with a tool called a stylus—they had no paper or pencils, and certainly no computers!*

1. In what ways were the early schools in Sumer similar to schools of today?

Similarities include: students did homework, recited lessons, and had tests. They

studied literature, mathematics, art, and religion.

2. In what ways were the early schools in Sumer different from schools of today?

Differences include: only boys attended school. They learned to do mathematics and

to write by copying. They used clay tablets instead of paper or computers.

B. Write a paragraph comparing and contrasting today's schooling with schooling in earlier times. For example, you might compare your grandparents' life with your own. What was the same? What was different?

Accept all appropriate responses. Answers should include details that describe their

comparisons. Instead of writing about themselves, students may compare the lives of

two other people.

Applying the Skill to Other Disciplines: Encourage students to use a Venn diagram when making comparisons in math, science, and social studies assignments.

Individualized Learning: Have students complete the page independently. Encourage students to use a Venn diagram, noting the ways in which schools in Sumer are similar to and different from schools today.

Student Self-Assessment: Ask students to rate themselves in the following areas on a scale of 1-4, with 1 being the least degree and 4 being the greatest degree: ability to utilize the strategy, ease in writing sidenotes, and ability to transfer skill to reading. (Make clear that student responses are for their own purposes only.)

To review

page 52

Key Words

Lesson Objective: To identify key words in the magazine articles and to connect them with familiar words by using a cluster diagram.

Oral Language: Invite students to name some key words related specifically to one of their subjects in school such as math, science, or physical education.

Introducing Strategies

When authors write articles, they use special words that are related to the subject of the article, called **key words.** Good readers look for key words in titles and subtitles before they read. They also make note of key words within the text as they read. To help them better understand articles, good readers think about other words they know that are related to the key words.

The cluster below shows how readers can connect words they know to key words in articles.

Modeling the Strategy: Use the students' textbook title or the title of the article about Laura Weber to model identifying key words and connecting them to familiar words. Show students how the cluster diagram can help them to identify key words and to make connections with familiar words. Adjust the Reproducible Activity Master on page T15 of the ATE to help students apply the cluster diagram strategy to "Laura Weber: One Native American Whose Business Is the Environment."

Reading the Newspaper Article

Reread the article about Laura Weber on pages 43-46. As you read, underline any key words. Think about what words you know that are related to these key words.

1. List some of the key words or phrases you underlined.

Accept reasonable responses which may include such words as *environmental crises,*

waste management, science, Native American, AISES, reduction, reusing, recycling.

_____

_____

2. Choose one of the key words you listed for #1. Write some words you know that are related to the key word.

Accept appropriate responses that indicate a connection between the related words

and the meaning of the key word as it is used in the article.

_____

_____

Practicing Key Words

A. The incomplete sentences below are about the article on Laura Weber. Circle the letter in front of the word or words that best complete the sentence. Then, on the lines provided, explain why you made the choice you did.

1. Words that could be considered key words in the article about Laura Weber are _____
    a. *garbage* and *criticism*.
    b. *management* and *process*.
    c. *environmental crises* and *waste management*.
    d. *business* and *Native American*.

   Students should suggest that they are *both* critical influences in Weber's life.

2. Knowing more about _____ would help a reader better understand the problems Laura Weber's company tries to solve.
    a. chemical engineering   c. geology
    b. turtles   d. waste management

   Students should suggest that the purpose of Weber's business is to help companies

   reduce the amount of garbage they produce.

3. Today Laura Weber is working very hard to reduce the need for _____
    a. research.   c. local government.
    b. landfills.   d. trees.

   Students may mention that reducing garbage is Weber's job.

B. Which of Laura Weber's three environmental Rs listed on page 46 is your school or community using? Write a paragraph describing what you are doing or would like to do. Underline the key words in your paragraph.

Accept all appropriate responses that relate local practices to Weber's 3Rs. Students

may choose to write solely about school or opportunities in the community.

Purpose: The purpose of the **Practicing** page is to help students practice the skill of identifying key words.

Peer Sharing: Have students complete Section A independently. Then have them work with a partner to compare answers. Encourage students to make sure their partners provide details from the article to support the choices they made.

Conferencing: Have students work with a peer to identify the key words in each other's responses.

Applying **Key Words**

Read the excerpt below from *The Poisons in Our Lives* in an article called "Hazardous Substances." Then answer the questions that follow.

Applying the Skill to Other Media:
Encourage students to identify and think about key words as they watch nature programs, news shows, or documentaries on television.

Cooperative Learning:
Have students work in pairs to complete the page. Suggest that they circle possible key words as they read the paragraph. Have students discuss their key words before they answer the first question. Tell students that there need not be a consensus on their responses. Students may continue to work together to answer the second question, although some students may prefer to work independently.

> *Do you have ammonia, floor polish, disinfectant, nail polish, paint, toothbrushes, or carpeting in your house? How about compact discs or audio tapes? . . . All of these things have something in common—they have been made using chemical technology. Just about everything in your life, from food to clothes to furniture, is produced with chemicals. Chemical technology has made possible many of the conveniences and benefits of modern life. But this technology also has a dangerous side. It uses and produces huge amounts of chemicals that are hazardous to human health and the environment.*

1. As you read, what key words, or words specific to the topic, did you identify?

Students may identify the words *chemical technology*, *chemicals*, and *environment*.
_____

2. Some communities do not have chemical waste collection days. Use some of the key words you identified to write a paragraph stating why your community should have a semi-annual chemical waste collection day.

Accept all reasonable responses. Some students may not agree that a semi-annual

chemical waste collection day is necessary. Make sure that students support their

responses with details about their own communities.
_____
_____
_____
_____
_____
_____
_____

To review
⬇
page 54

Janice Wolfinbarger Gay was born and raised on the Hupa Indian Reservation in Hoopa, California. Gay worked in market research and public relations before founding the Epilepsy Society of Southern New York. In talking to and writing about Laura Weber, Gay found herself wishing that she had known of similar Native American role models while growing up.

Laura Weber: One Native American Whose Business Is the Environment

by Janice Gay

Laura Weber may seem to be a very unlikely person to help cities and companies solve one of the nation's most severe environmental crises. Yet, she is doing just that.

In the process, this young Native American woman has managed to prove wrong the people who said she could never succeed because of poor grades. She used that criticism, along with a new understanding of her ethnic background, as driving forces to help her start her own waste management company.

Today Weber has degrees in chemistry and chemical engineering and a masters degree in civil and environmental engineering. Weber and her company, PM Earth, are in a position to help fight this country's war on garbage.

Cities are faced more and more with shrinking landfill space in which to put garbage. Large cities like New York, Los Angeles, and Chicago are all struggling with a big problem. They either have to add more landfill space, something that is very hard to do, or reduce the amount of trash that goes into the landfills.

That's not going to be easy. In 1990 alone, solid waste in the United States, if spread across a football field, would have created a mountain of trash 91.3 miles high. That's taller than 17 Mount Everests, the highest mountain in the world.

Weber Develops an Interest in Science

It might shock Weber's early teachers to know she has some answers to the problem.

"When I was in high school, I started to tell people I wanted to go to college," Weber told an interviewer from

Even though she wasn't successful in high school, Laura Weber kept trying. She is obviously very determined. Her determination to work hard and get a good education is something that stayed the same before and after college.

During her high school years she hated the sciences, but meeting Vera Cunningham sparked an interest in chemistry.

Making Predictions: Ask students to predict how poor grades might effect Laura Weber later in life.

Response Clue: Students may wonder how connecting with her heritage will change Laura Weber.

Laura Weber became involved in her Native American heritage and AISES when she was in college. Even though her background stayed the same, her involvement was one thing that changed. This makes me think about ways I've changed and ways I've stayed the same.

Winds of Change magazine in 1992. "They said, 'You'll never make it in college.'"

That's because her high school grades were barely average. Still, she was determined. She finally won acceptance into the University of New York at Plattsburgh, a small town on the shores of Lake Champlain near the Canadian border.

There she met Veronica Cunningham, a <u>chemistry</u> lab teacher, who sparked Weber's interest in <u>science</u>. Before that, Weber had always disliked this subject.

That's when the challenge really began.

Weber, born in 1961 in Omar, New York, had nearly flunked chemistry in high school. However, Cunningham showed her that science could be interesting. Weber decided she would like to study <u>chemical engineering</u>. But Plattsburgh did not offer a degree in this subject. So, with Cunningham's help, Weber became a student at Clarkson University about 75 miles from Plattsburgh. That school had an agreement that allowed students to study at Plattsburgh for three years, then at Clarkson for two. When Weber finished, she would have two degrees, one from each school.

But the studies at Clarkson were even more difficult than those at Plattsburgh.

"My grades actually got worse," Weber said. "I hung on by my fingernails."

Weber Connects with Her Mohawk Heritage

Even while Weber was struggling with grades, she was busy learning more about herself.

Although she has always known she is <u>Native American</u>, Weber knew almost nothing about her ethnic background. Still, she did recall that her relatives had come from Canada. She also knew she was a <u>Mohawk</u>, a Native American group from a region crossing the New York-Canadian border.

During her senior year at Clarkson, Weber talked with a career counselor. He noticed Weber's summer job as a bridge painter. The counselor told Weber that Mohawks, known for their ability to work high up on the steel skeletons of bridges and office buildings, had built the bridge. He then asked if she was a Mohawk. When Weber said yes, the counselor told her about a group for Native Americans interested in science and engineering.

The group, called the <u>American Indian Science and Engineering Society (AISES)</u>, would eventually support the dream that became Weber's career path. First, though, she had to tackle more school.

Weber was determined to go to graduate school to earn a master's degree. An advisor at Clarkson told her to forget it. Go into sales, he said. You'll never make it in graduate school.

But the dean at Clarkson thought Weber should be given a chance. She was allowed to attend the first semester of graduate school to see how well she could do. If she performed poorly, she would be out.

"It wasn't until graduate school that my grades really improved. All my life I had people telling me I couldn't do these things and I really wanted to prove to them that I could."

AISES Inspires Weber's Career

With her studies going well, Weber also became more involved with <u>AISES</u>. She attended a national AISES conference in Seattle, Washington, and was surprised by what she saw.

"There were 500 or 600 people there, but it all felt like a family. It really touched me. I connected with my heritage through that conference and the powwow."

(Modern Native Americans still hold powwows, large meetings at which traditional dances, storytelling, and displays are staged. These large meetings unite Native Americans from all over the United States and celebrate their cultures.)

Weber's new identification with Native Americans, who have traditionally valued nature, inspired her to look toward a career in which she could help the environment.

Weber next thought about moving to a city or staying in the Thousand Islands region of the St. Lawrence River area. (She had settled in this part of New York after marrying.) Weber decided to stay and open her own business.

Make your own notes about what changed and what remained the same from Laura Weber's early life to her later life. Write your notes in the margins.

Response Clue: Students may note examples on this page of Weber's determination as a constant in her life.

Response Clue: Students may note that AISES is a key word. Additional key words students may have identified are underlined on the ATE pages.

Cultural Awareness: Discuss with students the word *powwow*. Tell them that the original Indian word *Pauwau* referred to a medicine man, or shaman. Surrounded by well-wishers, the shaman would sing and dance during a healing. Today it generally refers to an important gathering or meeting to celebrate Native American culture and heritage.

Response Clue: Students' notes may reflect some of their own interests that developed from an awareness of their cultural heritage or family history.

PM Earth Deals with Landfill Problem

She called the new firm <u>PM Earth</u>, or <u>Preserve Mother Earth</u>. The name reflects Weber's understanding of Native American beliefs: People should respect the earth as they would respect their own mothers.

In addition, the logo for PM Earth is based on <u>Hupa</u> tradition. It shows a turtle with an image of North America on its back. The healthy turtle in the PM logo symbolizes a healthy <u>environment</u>.

Today Weber is doing her part to keep that turtle healthy. Her company works with corporations and local governments to help adopt Weber's "Three Rs."

These Rs are <u>reduction</u>, <u>reusing</u>, and <u>recycling</u>. According to Weber these actions can greatly reduce the need for <u>landfill</u> in this country. In fact, she argues, the three Rs can slash the 91-mile high mountain of trash to 11 miles, or just two Mount Everests.

First, she says, source reduction should be followed by all businesses. In other words, each company should work to buy fewer things that become waste. For example, companies can pressure suppliers to get rid of unnecessary packaging materials.

Second, after material is brought into a company and used, it is possible to reuse that same product. For example, some farmers have discovered paper that comes onto the farm as wrapping can later be used as livestock bedding.

Third, there is recycling, the process in which something is used to make a new product. Weber believes recycling can significantly reduce the number of new trees that must be cut or energy that must be used to make goods. Recycling can also ease the landfill crunch, since a bottle that is melted into something new isn't going to be put in a landfill.

Weber's job is to help companies put the three Rs into place. She and her company are very successful. But for Weber, there's more to her career than profit.

"The Creator has a path for us," she has said. "We should follow the Creator's path because he lets us know that everything happens for a reason."

In Weber's case, her early struggles in school and her new awareness of her background led her to an important career choice. She believes this proves that people should never lose faith in themselves.

"Always believe in yourself," she says. "If you have a goal, stick with it even if you feel you have no support from anyone. Just keep going."

Meeting Individual Needs: If students have trouble identifying key words, ask them which is more important to remember, the name of Weber's company or her three Rs.

ESL/LEP: Help students distinguish between the literal and idiomatic meanings of *crunch*.

Summarizing: Have students stop here to define the purpose of Weber's company by summarizing the three Rs.

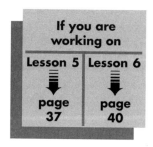

If you are working on

Lesson 5	Lesson 6
page 37	page 40

Arturo Gonzalez is a full-time journalist who specializes in personality profiles and travel articles. He is the San Diego correspondent for both *People* and *LIFE* magazines. He and his wife, Maureen, have about 3,000 bylines in major United States and overseas publications. They both enjoy baseball.

The Alomars–Baseball's Version of *All in the Family*

by Arturo and Maureen Gonzalez

There's an old saying, "like father, like son." In the case of the baseball-playing Alomar family of Salinas, Puerto Rico, it's "Like father, like son . . . like son."

The Alomars are big league baseball's version of *All in the Family*, with three family members of two generations starring in America's most popular game. Sandy, Sr., played for 15 years in major league baseball. He was a sure-footed infielder for half-a-dozen top teams. Now he coaches, instructing other young players the way he taught his own two boys.

His oldest son, Sandy, Jr., is an All-Star catcher for the Cleveland Indians. He was voted Rookie of the Year in his first season. The younger son, Roberto (called "Robbie" by his family), wears a chunky 1992 World Series ring. He is the All-Star second baseman for the World Champion Toronto Blue Jays. When the two Alomar boys played together in the 1991 All-Star Game, it was only the third time in history that two members of the same family were on an All-Star diamond together.

Together with the Padres in San Diego

For a brief period at the end of the 1980s, all three Alomars were wearing the same major league baseball uniforms. First they were with Charleston in the Class A minor leagues. Then they went to the San Diego Padres, a team that regularly turns up at the bottom of the National League West.

"We saw more of Dad with Charleston and the Padres than we had most of the years when we were growing up," Roberto recollects. "When we were kids going to school in Puerto Rico, Dad was away for eight months of every year on the mainland playing ball. During summer school vacations, we might be with him on the road for a while, but seldom for very long. We'd

The Alomars ■ **47**

Response Clue: Students may note that in contrast to Sandy and Roberto's early childhood, they spent a lot of time with their dad when all three of them were with Charleston and the San Diego Padres.

Making Predictions: Have students stop here to predict what they think will happen next to the brothers.

only really be with him full time from October through February—then it would be <u>spring training</u>, and he'd be gone again. The Padres period was great for us—but it didn't last very long."

Sandy, Jr., Makes a Move

Sandy, Jr., was the first Alomar to get traded from the Padres. A hefty 6'5", 200-pound catcher with a great arm, he had the bad luck to end up on the Padres team playing behind Benito Santiago. This fellow Latino <u>backstop</u> has the deadliest <u>catcher's arm</u> in baseball. As a result, Sandy, Jr., saw limited action, and in 1989, the Padres traded him to the <u>Indians</u>.

"Sure, the <u>trade</u> broke up our nice little Alomar family reunion in San Diego," Sandy, Jr., admits, "but it meant I got to play in the big leagues everyday, not just every once in a while. That's what any ball player really wants—to be out on the field every day."

Sandy, Jr.'s career in the big leagues has been good, but not sensational. Yes, there was the <u>1991 All Star</u> appearance, and the Rookie of the Year award, but he has experienced setbacks, too. Injuries have plagued Sandy, Jr. He has often suffered rotator cuff problems—a damaged muscle in his <u>throwing shoulder</u> which causes him pain and limits some movement.

Meeting Individual Needs: Have students stop at the end of this paragraph. Ask them to reread this one and the previous paragraph. As they look for key words, remind them that not all words specific to the subject are necessarily key words.

One of Sandy, Jr.'s earliest challenges in Cleveland was learning how to catch the very tricky <u>knuckleball.</u> This fluttering pitch comes in twisting and swerving, and usually makes the batter miss. It also can make an inexperienced <u>catcher</u> look foolish when it squirts away from him. To catch the famous <u>knucklers</u> of <u>ace Cleveland pitcher</u> Tom Candiotti, Sandy, Jr., had to use an oversized <u>mitt</u> for the first time. This meant he had to abandon his favorite glove, one which had been stitched back together countless times over many seasons.

Despite the pesky injuries, Sandy, Jr., is living up to the high expectations the <u>Indians' organization</u> has for him. Luis Isaac, a veteran <u>coach</u> in the Cleveland <u>bullpen</u>, says flatly, "Sandy Alomar is the best catching prospect I've seen since Johnny Bench. You wait and see how he develops as a hitter. He still has some baby fat. Most Latin players don't mature until their late twenties." At 27, Sandy, Jr., is just entering his prime.

Robbie Moves to Canada

If little brother Robbie is better known than his older brother, it's primarily because of the epic <u>pennant,</u>

Additional Skills: This selection is also appropriate for teaching strategies for Identifying Fact and Opinion (see ATE pages 60-62).

playoff, and World Series achievements of the Toronto Blue Jays at the end of their exciting 1992 season. When Toronto became the first Canadian team ever to win the World Series, Robbie emerged as one of the town's favorite sons—more famous even than most of the local Maple Leaf hockey stars. When a Puerto Rican who plays on grass outshines Canadians who play on ice—in Canada—he's got to be something very special.

And he is. Roberto was, happily for him, traded from the tail-end Padres in 1991. His new Toronto team was gathering itself for a run at World Series fame. Robbie took over the second base slot, and became the glue that held the infield together.

His first few games were a statistical disaster. Always a super "glove man," able to scoop up the toughest grounders, he piled up 11 errors in his first month of play. His mistakes occurred not because he was butter-fingered, but because he was trying to run down every single ball hit anywhere near him. Elusive grounders were just glancing off his outstretched glove time after time. After settling in, however, Roberto learned how to move a few steps this way or that, depending on the batter and how he was being pitched to. As a result, yesterday's errors have almost all turned into today's outs.

Roberto is also an incredible base runner—stealing 49 bases one year, including 17 in a row. "He puts pressure on the other team in so many different ways," a Jays coach reveals. At the plate in 1992, he batted .310, an average that rocketed to an impressive .345 with men in scoring position. And he himself scored 105 runs.

Chito Gaston, the Blue Jays' manager, says simply, "Robbie Alomar is the most selfless player I've ever come across in baseball." Adds Alomar's teammate, Mookie Wilson, "Robbie plays all out, all the time." Aging superstar Dave Winfield insists, "Right now, Robbie could become Canada's Prime Minister if he'd be willing to run for election."

Robbie's so devoted to baseball that in Toronto he lives at the ballpark—literally. Toronto's modern, futuristic SkyDome baseball stadium has a hotel built into its right-field grandstand. Robbie lives in a two-room suite in this hotel for the entire season. "No, my suite doesn't overlook the field," he admits. "I have a parking lot view. I want to get away from baseball when I'm home."

Clarification: Have students go back over the selection and skim for information about Sandy's career. Tell them that keeping this information in mind as they read about Roberto will help them make comparisons among the Alomar brothers more easily.

ESL/LEP: Discuss the meaning of *tail-end* and the ways in which this change was particularly important to Roberto's career.

Meeting Individual Needs: This paragraph offers another opportunity to help specific students who are having trouble making comparisons. Have them compare and contrast Roberto's first few games with his games after he settled in.

Response Clue: Students may note that while Sandy was a good catcher, he had several injuries and needed time to mature. Robbie, on the other hand, as a second-baseman for the Toronto Blue Jays, became an incredible base runner.

Sometimes after a game, Robbie is showered and walking back to his suite even before the spectators who have been watching the game have started heading for the elevators. They pass this tall Latino in the corridor without realizing that, just a few minutes before, they were cheering for his diving catches and daring base running.

Robbie may be the only ball player in the world who can play a hometown series and never go out doors from the beginning of the week to the end. The stadium boasts an 11,000-ton sliding roof which can be closed during wet or snowy weather. So Robbie often plays under a roof, then goes home to his hotel suite without ever leaving the structure.

"It's too much trouble to go out and get a life of my own," the 25-year-old bachelor insists. "You have to rent or buy a place, go look for rugs and furniture, get cable TV hooked up. The suite suits me fine. I get all the TV I want. Need food? Call room service. Need laundry or pressing? Call housekeeping."

And he can afford it. The Blue Jays have given Roberto Alomar a four-year, $18.5 million contract. This makes him the second best-paid second baseman in baseball, several million dollars behind longtime star Ryne Sandberg.

Alomar is clearly the game's best second baseman,

Response Clue: Students responses should continue to compare and contrast the careers of Sandy and Robbie Alomar.

and he's steadily improving. His smarts on the field belie his relatively short major league career. "He seems like he's about 30," complains long time rival, the <u>Oakland A's</u> Carney Lansford. "He looks so experienced up there at the plate. You never expect him to take a bad swing." And when he does, he is his own harshest critic. Robbie's been known to take an extra half-hour of strenuous batting practice after a game in which he feels he's hit the ball poorly.

"For him to have accomplished what he has at his age is really mind-boggling," says Larry Hisle, the Jays' batting coach. "You have to remember that most players his age are just making it to the big leagues. Robbie has already been an All Star—twice."

You Never Know When You Might Face an Alomar!

Being sons of a big league father produces some rather interesting situations for the Alomars who now find themselves in the big leagues. For example, Robbie remembers meeting one of his father's teammates, a pitcher named Nolan Ryan. A decade-and-a-half later, Robbie got his first <u>big league hit off</u> this same Nolan Ryan. And when Ryan recently tossed his epic seventh <u>no-hit game</u>, guess who was the game's last out? You got it—Robbie Alomar.

Neither of the younger Alomars has settled down yet to get married and raise a family, much to mother Maria's disappointment. If they do, and have sons—who knows— maybe there will be three generations of Alomars in the majors one day.

Additional Skills: This selection is also appropriate for teaching strategies for using Context Clues. For example, students can use context clues to understand the meaning of the unfamiliar word *belie*. (See ATE pages 5-7.)

Response Clue: Students may note the accomplishments of Roberto compared to Sandy's relatively new career in which he is "just entering his prime."

If you are working on

Lesson 5	Lesson 6
⬇	⬇
page 52	page 54

Reviewing *Compare* and *Contrast*

Reviewing the Strategy: To complete the Venn diagram, have students refer to the sidenotes they wrote on pages 47-51.

A. Read the newspaper article "The Alomars—Baseball's Version of *All in the Family*" on pages 47-51. As you read, make notes that compare and contrast the Alomar brothers' baseball careers. Then organize your sidenotes by completing the diagram below.

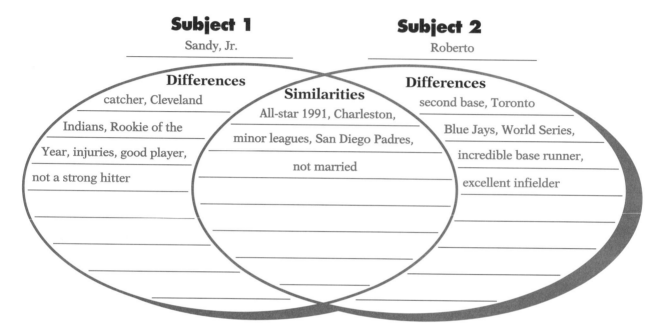

Subject 1
Sandy, Jr.

Subject 2
Roberto

Differences
catcher, Cleveland
Indians, Rookie of the
Year, injuries, good player,
not a strong hitter

Similarities
All-star 1991, Charleston,
minor leagues, San Diego Padres,
not married

Differences
second base, Toronto
Blue Jays, World Series,
incredible base runner,
excellent infielder

Managing the Lesson: Answers in the Venn diagram are suggestions. Students may find other similarities and differences between the Alomar brothers such as: Roberto is probably better known than Sandy because of the World Series achievements of the Toronto Blue Jays in 1992.

Peer Sharing: Suggest that students with similar predictions work together to make their comparisons.

B. What do you think the future holds for the Alomar brothers? Use details from your diagram to make a prediction about each brother. Then compare your predictions about Sandy's and Roberto's careers.

Accept reasonable responses based on details supplied in students' diagrams. They

may predict that Roberto will always be more successful or that as he reaches prime,

Sandy will catch up.

Testing Compare and Contrast

A. The sentences below are about the article "The Alomars—Baseball's Version of *All in the Family*." Mark each statement true (T) or false (F). Then on the lines provided, rewrite each sentence you marked false to make it true. Give details that support each sentence you marked true.

Test-Taking Hints: Remind students to read each statement carefully. Explain that just because part of a statement is true doesn't mean the entire sentence is true.

___F___ **1.** One way Sandy and Roberto are alike is that they both play for the Toronto Blue Jays.

Roberto plays for the Toronto Blue Jays, but Sandy plays for the Cleveland Indians.

Meeting Individual Needs: Have students indicate the places in the text where the details support their revised statements.

___F___ **2.** Another way Sandy and Roberto are alike is that both have had impressive batting averages.

Roberto has an impressive batting average, while Sandy is still developing as a hitter.

___T___ **3.** The Alomar brothers play different positions: Roberto plays second base. Sandy is a catcher.

Roberto plays second base for the Toronto Blue Jays; Sandy catches for the

Cleveland Indians.

___F___ **4.** Both brothers were named Rookie of the Year in the same year.

only Sandy was named Rookie of the Year in 1991.

B. Write a paragraph comparing and contrasting two very different characters that you have seen in recent movies or on TV. How are they similar? How are they different?

Accept appropriate responses. Encourage students to keep the two questions in mind

and give details that support their comparisons.

Assessing Student Writing: Rate student writing on a scale of 1-4, with 1 being the least degree and 4 being the greatest degree. Use the following criteria: originality, organization, reasoning, and clarity.

To begin Lesson 6

page 40

Reviewing **Key Words**

Reviewing the Strategy: To complete the word cluster, have students refer to the words they underlined in the article. Tell them to choose three of these key words and write them on the diagram before writing the related words.

A. Reread the article "The Alomars—Baseball's Version of *All in the Family*" on pages 47-51. As you read, underline key words you identify. Use some of the words as you complete the chart below.

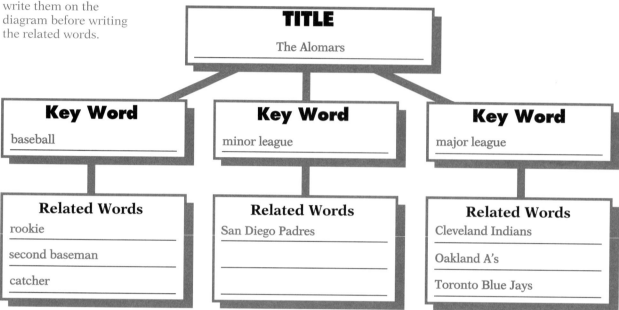

TITLE
The Alomars

Key Word
baseball

Key Word
minor league

Key Word
major league

Related Words
rookie
second baseman
catcher

Related Words
San Diego Padres

Related Words
Cleveland Indians
Oakland A's
Toronto Blue Jays

Managing the Lesson: Answers in the cluster are suggestions. Students may find additional key words such as *knuckleball, World Series,* or *base runner.*

Peer Sharing: Suggest that students work in pairs or small groups and brainstorm words. Then they can separate out the words they think are key words.

Writing Process: Students might like to develop their key words into a paragraph describing their particular interests.

B. Think about something you are interested in. Is it music? sports? fashion? List as many *key words* as you can think of related to your area of interest.

Accept all responses that are related to a specific subject or topic.

_____

_____

_____

_____

_____

_____

_____

_____

_____

_____

_____

Lesson 6	Introducing page 40	Practicing page 41	Applying page 42	Reviewing page 54	Testing page 55

Testing Key Words

A. The sentences below are from the article about the Alomar brothers. Read each sentence. Circle the letter in front of the key word or words in that sentence. Then, on the lines provided, explain why you made that choice. Note that more than one choice may be correct.

1. "His oldest son, Sandy, Jr., . . . was voted Rookie of the Year in his first season."

   a. son   c. season
   (b.) Rookie of the Year   d. voted

The phrase tells something about Sandy, Jr.

2. "A hefty 6'5", 200-pound catcher with a great arm, he had the bad luck to end up on the Padres team playing behind Benito Santiago."

   (a.) catcher   c. luck
   b. arm   d. team

Students may suggest the other choices could refer to many subjects.

3. "Roberto was . . . traded. . . . His new Toronto team was gathering itself for a run at World Series fame."

   (a.) Toronto   (c.) traded
   (b.) World Series   d. fame

Students may suggest these words explain something about Roberto's new team.

4. "Roberto is also an incredible base-runner—stealing 49 bases one year, including 17 in a row."

   (a.) base-runner   c. stealing
   b. year   d. row

Students may suggest the term best describes Roberto.

B. Describe an experience you have had playing or watching baseball. Use some of the key words you remember from the article in your description.

Accept appropriate responses. If students have had no experience with baseball,

suggest they write about another sport or game. Ask students to underline the key

words they use in their paragraph.

_____

_____

_____

_____

Test-Taking Hints: Remind students to read the statement and all the choices thoroughly before answering. Tell them that more than one choice may be correct.

Meeting Individual Needs: Suggest that students review the selection by skimming it and noting the key words they underlined. Have them discuss why they think each is a key word.

Unit FOUR

BECOMING AN ACTIVE READER

Good readers are active readers. If they become confused while reading **magazine articles**, they stop, go back, and carefully reread a difficult passage. Rereading often clears up confusions.

Using Skills and Strategies

Identifying the most important ideas will help you keep track of information in articles. After identifying a **main idea,** look for **details** that give more information about it. To find main ideas and details, it may be helpful to ask yourself these questions: If I were telling a friend about the article, which major ideas would I be sure to include? Are there any important details that I should mention?

Learning to separate **statements of fact** from **statements of opinion** will help you read articles actively. You may ask: Does this sentence state a fact? Why is the author including it? Does the statement give the writer's—or someone else's—opinions? Do I agree or disagree? What do I already know that would help me decide?

In this unit, identifying **main ideas and details** and separating **statements of fact** from **statements of opinion** will help you become an active reader.

The Magazine Article: The Writer's Voice

The range of subject matter found in magazine articles reflects the diversity of American life. Reading articles about your favorite subject—whether it is cars, current events, television shows, or cooking—can give you information on a topic that interests you.

Responding to Magazine Articles

It is helpful to jot down what you are learning as you read "Gloria Estefan: Her Remarkable Recovery" and "Rap Music: What's It All About?" Writing sidenotes will help you remember the articles.

Unit Enrichment:
Have small groups of students create rap lyrics based on something they have read. Students can present their rap music to the whole class, tape record it, or both.

Main Ideas and Details

| *Lesson 7* | Introducing *page 57* | Practicing *page 58* | Applying *page 59* | Reviewing *page 73* | Testing *page 74* |

Introducing Strategies

Main ideas are the most important ideas in an article. Main ideas are usually supported by **details**—facts that tell who, what, where, why, and when. Sometimes a main idea is stated directly in a topic sentence. Other times, the main idea is suggested but not stated directly. One way good readers identify main ideas and details is by asking, "What are the major points that the author is making? What are some facts that support these ideas?"

The chart below is one way readers can organize main ideas and details as they read.

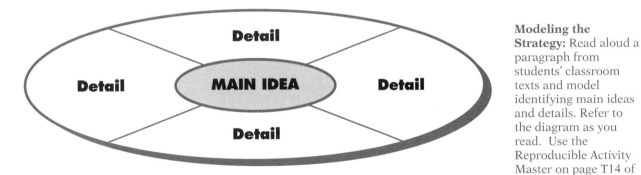

Reading the Magazine Article

Read the magazine article "Gloria Estefan: Her Remarkable Recovery" on pages 63-67 and the sidenotes on pages 63 and 64. The sidenotes show how one good reader identified main ideas and details in the article. After reading, complete the items below.

1. List two important ideas the reader learned about Gloria Estefan's life.

Ideas may include: Gloria's interest in music developed early; a serious accident nearly

ended her career; she made a remarkable recovery; her career is booming again.

2. Choose one of the main ideas and write some details that tell more about it.

Responses should include story details that support the main idea. For example,

Estefan's accident occurred on March 20, 1990, and the impact smashed two

vertebrae in the middle of her back.

ESL/LEP: Make available the song lyrics and a tape of one of Gloria Estefan's recordings for students to read and listen to. Ask students to choose one of the songs and to discuss with a peer what it is about.

Modeling the Strategy: Read aloud a paragraph from students' classroom texts and model identifying main ideas and details. Refer to the diagram as you read. Use the Reproducible Activity Master on page T14 of the ATE to help students apply the strategy to "Gloria Estefan: Her Remarkable Recovery."

Managing the Lesson: Remind students to use the sidenotes on pages 63-64 to complete items 1 and 2. The sidenotes model the skill of identifying main ideas and details.

Lesson 7	Introducing page 57	Practicing page 58	Applying page 59	Reviewing page 73	Testing page 74

Practicing *Main Ideas and Details*

A. The questions below are based on the article "Gloria Estefan: Her Remarkable Recovery" on pages 63-67. Circle the letter before the best answer. Then explain the reasons for your choice on the lines provided.

1. If you were telling a friend about Gloria Estefan's life, which of these main ideas would you be sure to include?
   a. Estefan's mother was a school teacher.
   b. The Bay of Pigs invasion failed.
   c. Estefan has made a remarkable recovery after her accident, and today her career is flourishing.
   d. "Rhythm Is Gonna Get You" is the name of a song recorded by The Miami Sound Machine.

Only this item makes an overall, general statement about Gloria Estefan's life. The
other answers are less important details.

2. Which of the following statements is not a detail?
   a. Estefan was born in Havana in 1958.
   b. When she was 11, she helped care for her invalid father.
   c. At a young age, she began to develop her musical talent.
   d. Estefan's success is due to talent, perseverance, and courage.

This statement is a summary of a main idea in the article.

B. Write about a main idea in the article that impressed you as you read. Explain why it stood out. Include details from the article to support your response.

Accept all appropriate responses that include a main idea and supporting details from
the article. Students may suggest that Estefan's recovery impressed them. She
underwent daily physical therapy, wrote songs, and has been active in social causes.

Purpose: The purpose of the **Practicing** page is to help students practice the skill of identifying main ideas and details. Questions reflect the strategy shown in the graphic organizer on the **Introducing** page.

Peer Sharing: Have students complete section A independently. Then ask them to work with a partner to compare their answers. Encourage students to make sure their partners provide reasons that support their answers.

Conferencing: Have students work with a peer to identify the main idea and supporting details in each other's responses. Students can complete a diagram like the one on the **Introducing** page to show their main idea and details.

Applying **Main Ideas and Details**

Read the article below about Habitat for Humanity. Then answer the questions that follow.

HABITAT FOR HUMANITY:
Making Dreams Come True

Habitat for Humanity is a non-profit organization dedicated to combating homelessness throughout the world. Using volunteer labor and donated materials, Habitat for Humanity has built or renovated over 6,500 homes since 1976. The homes are for people who would not otherwise be able to afford them. The new owners must make small monthly mortgage payments and volunteer 500 hours of their labor on other Habitat homes.

Two of the most enthusiastic and famous volunteers are former President Jimmy Carter and his wife Rosalynn. Each of them spends time each year building Habitat housing. In addition, Jimmy Carter has served as director of the organization. Mrs. Carter has been an advisor to the group.

1. Write a sentence that tells the main idea of the first paragraph.

Habitat for Humanity is a nonprofit organization that builds houses for people who
can't afford them.

2. What is the main idea of the second paragraph?

President Carter and his wife Rosalynn support Habitat for Humanity.

3. Select one of the main ideas you have identified and give details that support it.

Responses should include selection details that support the main idea. Students may
discuss that Habitat for Humanity uses volunteers to build or renovate homes, and
that new owners must make small payments and volunteer their time for other
renovations.

Applying the Skill to Everyday Reading: Have students select articles from a newspaper and identify main ideas and details. Ask them to write a summary of the article and to underline the most important idea in their summary paragraph.

Meeting Individual Needs: Help students identify the main ideas by explaining that in this article, the first sentence in each paragraph states its main idea. Ask students to underline these sentences.

Cooperative Learning: Have students complete the page in groups of three. Make sure that each student in the group has a chance to contribute. Have groups present their answers to the class.

Assessing Cooperative Work: As you observe groups, note the degree to which members listen to each other, contribute to the discussion, and add relevant information. Then have each group member rate his or her performance.

To review

page 73

Fact and Opinion

Lesson Objective: To respond to and distinguish facts from opinions by identifying statements that can be proved and statements that express someone's belief or judgment.

Oral Language: Have each student tell a classmate about their favorite book or movie. Encourage students to tell some facts about it, such as who the characters are or what the setting is. Then they can give their opinions about why they liked the book or movie. Encourage students to respond to their partner's opinions.

Modeling the Strategy: Use a simple example of a fact or opinion to show how the diagram might be completed. For example, use statements such as: Mark Twain wrote *The Adventures of Tom Sawyer* in 1876; or *The Adventures of Tom Sawyer* is the most popular book ever written. Use the Reproducible Activity Master on page T14 of the ATE to help students apply the strategy to "Gloria Estefan: Her Remarkable Recovery."

Managing the Lesson: Remind students to use the words they circled and underlined when they reread the selection to complete items 1 and 2.

Lesson 8	Introducing *page 60*	Practicing *page 61*	Applying *page 62*	Reviewing *page 75*	Testing *page 76*

Introducing Strategies

In articles, writers often present **facts** along with their own **opinions** about a topic. A fact is a statement that can be proved to be true or false. An opinion is a statement that expresses someone's belief or judgment. Words such as *best, worse,* or *most popular,* may signal an opinion. Other words such as *remarkable* or *significant* tell the reader that the writer is making a judgment. Good readers agree or disagree with opinions in an article based on what they know about the topic.

The chart below shows how good readers think about statements of fact and opinion when reading articles.

Statement	Is It Fact or Opinion?	Reader's Response to Statement

Reading the Magazine Article

Reread the article "Gloria Estefan: Her Remarkable Recovery" on pages 63-67. As you read, underline statements of fact and circle statements of opinion.

1. List two facts from the article about Gloria Estefan's life. Explain how you can tell they are facts.

Students may suggest Estefan's birth date, her father's name, the groups that she sang with, and her album titles are facts because they can be proved.

2. Write two opinions from the article. Explain if you agree or disagree with each one.

Students may suggest that the statement that Estefan is adored and envied by thousands of people and that she was the spark that the Miami Sound Machine needed are opinions because they express judgments.

Practicing *Fact and Opinion*

A. Each pair of statements contains a statement of fact and a statement of opinion. Next to each statement write F for fact or O for opinion. Explain your choices on the lines provided.

1. F In 1990, Estefan's tour bus was hit by a truck.

O Estefan's remarkable story began in Havana.

The first statement can be proved true or false by reading a newspaper account of the

accident. In the second statement, the word *remarkable* signals a judgment.

2. O Gloria suffered what must have been unspeakable pain.

F Two vertebrae in the middle of Estefan's back were smashed.

In the first statement, the word *unspeakable* signals a judgment. The second statement

can be proved true or false.

3. F Estefan's record *Mi Tierra* was recorded entirely in Spanish.

O Estefan is the most popular Latin singer today.

The first statement can be proved true or false by listening to the record. The words

the most popular in the second statement signal an opinion.

B. Think of a performer whose music you enjoy listening to. Write a paragraph about that person. Include interesting facts as well as your own opinions about your subject.

Students should present facts and opinions about a favorite performer. Facts might

include dates, names of recordings and musicians, and record sales. Opinions might

include judgments of the musician's work.

_____

_____

_____

_____

_____

_____

_____

Purpose: The purpose of the **Practicing** page is to help students practice the skill of identifying fact and opinion. Questions reflect this strategy, which is explained on the **Introducing** page.

Individualized Learning: Have students complete the page independently. Make sure that they have explained how they determined if each statement was a fact or an opinion.

Conferencing: Have students work with a peer. Ask them to exchange paragraphs and try to identify statements of fact and statements of opinion in each other's work.

Assessing Student Writing: Rate each student's paragraph on a scale of 1-4, with 1 being the least degree and 4 being the greatest degree. Use the following criteria: uses statements of fact and statements of opinion, develops ideas logically through main ideas and details, and uses a magazine style.

Applying *Fact and Opinion*

As you read the article below, think about which statements are facts and which are opinions. Then complete the items that follow.

KRISTI YAMAGUCHI:
Gold on Ice

Kristi Yamaguchi won a gold medal for figure skating in the 1992 Olympics. Today she skates professionally, performing in such events as "Skates of Gold," a show featuring past gold medalists.

Kristi is wonderful to watch since she turned pro. She skates to more contemporary music. She has even used a hip-hop number by En Vogue. She also says she can have more fun with her costumes. "As an amateur, they tell you that your costume should go with the music and the program. If they think it takes away from the skating, they can actually penalize you."

1. List two statements of fact about Kristi Yamaguchi and explain how you could prove they were true.

Students may mention that the facts that Kristi Yamaguchi won a gold medal; that

today she skates professionally; and that she skated to a hip-hop number can be

proved true or false.

2. List a statement of opinion from the article. What made you decide it was an opinion instead of a fact?

Students may answer: "Kristi is wonderful to watch," and explain that the word

wonderful signals a judgment.

3. How did you respond to the statement of opinion that you listed above?

Responses should reflect an evaluation of the opinion. Students may have seen

Yamaguchi skate and agree with this judgment.

To review

page
75

Preteaching Vocabulary: You may wish to preteach the following words: *invalid, percussionist, vertebrae, physical therapy.*

Making Predictions: You may wish to have students predict what the article will be about after reading the title and headnote.

When newspaper reporter Fernando Romero writes about music, he relies on his own experiences. From the mid-1960s to 1983, Romero was a drummer for dozens of Latino, rock, and jazz groups. He quit drumming to become a newspaper reporter. His work often focuses on issues concerning the border between the United States and Mexico.

Gloria Estefan: Her Remarkable Recovery

by Fernando Romero

In 1993, at the age of 35, singer Gloria Estefan is adored and envied by thousands of people. She seems to be where most people only dream of being—on top of the world. And she's often on the top of pop music charts, too. Gloria herself has reason to feel good about where she is. Only three years before, in 1990, Gloria Estefan nearly lost her life. A horrifying tour-bus accident in March of that year was the cause.

On the Road to Success

Estefan's remarkable story began in Havana, where she was born in 1958. Her father, José Manuel Fajardo, was a bodyguard for Cuban dictator Fulgencio Batista. Her mother was a schoolteacher. At the end of 1958, Estefan's family fled to Miami. They were escaping the government of Fidel Castro, a Communist who had gained control of Cuba.

In 1961, Estefan's father participated in an attempt to rid Cuba of Castro's regime. The attack, known as the Bay of Pigs invasion, failed. He and other participants were jailed in Cuba. They remained there for two years until U.S. President John F. Kennedy secured their freedom. Later, Fajardo joined the U.S. Army and served in Vietnam. In 1968, he developed a disease of the brain and nervous system that made him an invalid. Gloria, 11 years old at the time, helped to care for her father until he was hospitalized in 1976. He died in 1980. Her father's disease was frightening to Gloria. She became very afraid of some day becoming an invalid herself.

During the years of her father's illness, Gloria must have needed something to help take her mind off his suffering. Perhaps that's why she wrapped herself in music. At a young age, she began developing her singing

The notes in the margins on pages 63 and 64 show how one reader identified main ideas and details.

Response Clue: Circles reflect opinions and underlinings reflect facts that students may have identified in the text.

◀ The main idea of this paragraph isn't stated directly. I believe it's that Gloria Estefan is successful today—and should feel good about it—because she made a major comeback after a near-fatal accident three years ago.

Response Clue: Students may have noted that the words *adored* and *envied* in the first paragraph signal opinions. Also, the first sentence in this paragraph contains both an opinion and a fact. Ask students to share their responses to the opinion.

Response Clue: Point out to students that section headings can help them identify main ideas in the article.

◀ I guess the main idea here is that Gloria's father's illness influenced her career.

Cultural Awareness: Have students share with the class some traditional songs from their own cultures.

ESL/LEP: Use a map or globe to show students the location of Miami, Florida; Cuba; and Lebanon.

The main idea here is that Gloria was successful as a singer, wife, and parent. The article tells us that the Miami Sound Machine was a hit; she married Emilio Estefan; and they had a baby boy, Nayib. These are details that support the main idea.

The words *national recognition, big break,* and *international fame* also support the idea that she was a success.

Write your own sidenotes as you read the rest of the article. Point out examples of main ideas and their supporting details.

Response Clue: Students may have underlined the titles of hit songs, the number of albums, and the dates to show facts. Students may also have noted how they would go about checking whether the facts are true.

talent. She especially loved Cuban music. In 1975, she joined a group called the Miami Latin Boys. Soon, they renamed themselves the Miami Sound Machine. The group featured horn and drum sections that played Cuban-inspired dance music. Gloria sang in both English and Spanish. One of the group's members was Emilio Estefan, a percussionist. Like Gloria, Emilio was born in Cuba. He was of Cuban and Lebanese heritage. Gloria and Emilio began dating, and in 1978 they were married. Three years later, they had a baby boy. They named him Nayib, in honor of Emilio's Lebanese heritage.

▶ By that time, the group was having the sort of tremendous success that most young groups can only hope for. They were popular in the Miami area and throughout Latin America. Gloria Estefan had become the group's unquestioned leader—that spark that every great group needs. Her beautiful, mellow, rich voice was wonderfully matched by the group's Latin-tinged arrangements. The Miami Sound Machine's distinctive sound was soon to bring it national recognition. The group's big break came in 1985, when one of its recordings, "Conga," reached the Top 10. Now Estefan

▶ and her group were on their way to international fame.

Other hits followed: "Rhythm Is Gonna Get You," "Don't Wanna Lose You," "Can't Stay Away from You," and "Bad Boy." In all, Estefan and the Miami Sound Machine sold about 9 million albums between 1985 and 1991 in the United States alone. By any standards, those were superstar numbers.

Estefan felt that things couldn't get better. Her personal life was stable. Nayib and Emilio traveled everywhere with Gloria. She loved her family, and she loved her work. Things seemed complete.

Tragedy Strikes

Suddenly, on March 20, 1990, Estefan's world shattered. On an icy road outside Tobyhanna, Pennsylvania, her tour bus, which was stopped because a jackknifed tractor-trailer was blocking the way, was rammed from the rear by a speeding truck. Aboard the demolished bus were Gloria, Emilio, Nayib and his tutor, and two band members.

The force of the crash knocked Emilio out of his laced tennis shoes and broke Nayib's collarbone. Gloria was jolted off a couch and slammed to the floor. The impact smashed two vertebrae in the middle of her back. Her injuries were so severe that doctors predicted her recovery could take years. It seemed that Gloria's fears about becoming an invalid might come true. Yet, she was determined to come out of the ordeal in good shape.

On the Road to Recovery

Gloria suffered what must have been unspeakable pain as a result of the injuries. She went through several operations involving a bone graft from her hip and the insertion of two metal rods, four brackets, and screws in her back to prop up the damaged vertebrae. In a 1991 interview, Emilio recalled his wife's agony and her strength in the face of it: "She was in pain so much of the time, but she'd never complain. Not once. I have never seen anyone do that in my whole life. I'd see her, and she would have tears in her eyes from pain, but she'd never complain. Knowing her, I'm not surprised by any of this. She's very committed, and I admire that very much."

During the first four months following the crash, the singer refused to think about performing again. "I just wanted to be a normal person once more. I just wanted to be able to walk and dress myself and tie my own shoes," she would say later. "But once my body started to respond, I decided that I never wanted to be less than I was before. It was important to me that I go beyond what I did in the past just to prove to myself that I could. For me, I had to do more just to tell myself that I'm OK." It must have been Gloria's determination that ultimately helped her heal faster than anyone, including the doctors, had predicted.

During her recovery—which included daily physical therapy sessions—Estefan spent her time writing songs. At the time, she surely couldn't have imagined that they would become the foundation of one of her most successful albums, *Into the Light.* She began production on this album an amazing six months after the crash. It includes a hit single, "Coming Out of the Dark," that is most representative of her recovery period. The name of the song came from a phrase her husband used as she was being flown by helicopter from one hospital to another. "We were being transported to this hospital, and [Emilio] saw the sun peeking out from behind these clouds," she says. "Feeling so desperate at the moment, all he could think of was wanting time to go by quickly and to have this behind us. And the line 'coming out of the dark' came to him." The music for the song includes a back-up gospel church choir. "Gospel music is born of a

Response Clue: Students may have noted that the fourth sentence in this paragraph is a statement of fact that also contains an opinion. It is a fact that the doctors made a prediction. However, the length of time they predicted—several years—is an opinion.

Response Clue: Ask students which sentence best states the main idea of this paragraph.

Clarification: Have students reread this paragraph to clarify Estefan's state of mind during the early stages of her recovery.

Gloria Estefan: Her Remarkable Recovery ■ **65**

lot of pain and suffering, and yet it is such a joyous and celebratory kind of music," Gloria explains.

Into the Light also features Latin, rhythm and blues, and soul music. Since its release in February 1991, the album has sold more than one million copies.

Looking Ahead

Gloria Estefan's recovery from her accident brought with it a change in how she views the world. Although she has always been aware of political and social events in the world, Gloria evidently now feels a need to be personally involved. Since her accident, she feels a keen responsibility to help ease the suffering of those she views as less fortunate than herself.

In 1992, Estefan attended the United Nations Conference on Human Rights as one of four U.S. delegates. She also was one of several entertainers who helped in the relief efforts for the victims of Hurricane Andrew. This hurricane destroyed the town of Homestead, Florida. Estefan spent countless hours distributing food and clothing to the victims. She also held a benefit concert for hurricane relief. In addition, she launched a new video, "Always Tomorrow," the proceeds of which went to help the victims.

Estefan has plunged into her career with seemingly limitless energy. She wants to make a movie and is searching through dozens of scripts for the right one. Meanwhile, she is busy recording and touring. Her 1993 album, *Mi Tierra (My Land)*, represents a return to Gloria's musical roots. Recorded entirely in Spanish, the album affirms her heritage. Within a few weeks of its release, the album was in the Top 30. This is one of the fastest rises ever for an album. To those who are watching the rousing comeback of Latin music, Gloria Estefan has to be viewed as the leader. She is in very good company, however. Exciting Latin artists such as Mexican balladeer Luis Miguel, the East Los Angeles Mex-rock band Los Lobos, superstar Linda Ronstadt, and rappers Mellow Man, Ace, Gerardo, and Frost are also popular 1990s voices for the Latin sound.

Despite her many activities and commitments, Gloria still seems to find time to slow down and remember what's most important about life. As she says, "Really, I just want to live to an old age and be healthy."

Response Clue: Students may have noted the word *seemingly* in the first sentence indicates that the author is expressing his opinion.

Cultural Awareness: Have students identify popular performers from their own cultures and tell something about them to the class.

If you are working on

Lesson 7	Lesson 8
↓	↓
page 57	page 60

Ron Harris has been a journalist for more than 17 years. He has received numerous awards for his writing, including one from the National Association of Black Journalists. Currently, Harris writes a weekly column for the *Los Angeles Times* covering issues and trends in southern California. Rap music is one musical trend that Harris has observed. He reports on its beginnings in the article below.

Rap Music: What's It All About?

by Ron Harris

It was 1979, and on the radio, in dance clubs, and at house parties across the United States, people began to hear something unique and exciting in their music.

What they heard was a record featuring three teenagers talking in rhyme and rhythm to the music of a popular recording called "Good Times." They were listening to a song called "Rapper's Delight." Nobody realized it then, but listeners were experiencing the birth of a new music form—rap music.

Since those days, rap has become a solid part of the U.S. music scene—right up there with blues, jazz, rock, rhythm and blues, and country and western. Sales of rap records total in the hundreds of millions of dollars. Rap music is heard on radio, in night clubs, in concerts, on TV, and in commercials selling everything from sodas to video games to hamburgers to athletic shoes.

What Is Rap Music?

Author David Troop describes rap in his book *The Attack* as "rhythmic talking over a funky beat." That is a good beginning, but rap is much more than that.

The term *rap* originated as African American street slang for the word *talk*. "Rapping with a friend," meant talking with a friend. Since this music form featured talking instead of singing, it was called rap music. The people who made the music were called rappers.

Since rap's beginnings, rappers have tended to talk about serious topics—urban problems such as gangs, crime, and drug abuse. The talk is not always clean, and many critics feel the songs promote violence. In fact, rap has been labeled as the African American version of heavy metal—a hard-rock type of music popular among some groups of young people. However, although the nature of the lyrics might be similar, the stories being told are quite different.

The music for rap is different, too. One of the most commonly used musical techniques is called sampling. While other songwriters compose original music to go with their lyrics, rappers create the music for their records by taking samples, or bits of music from other previously released records. For example, rappers may use the drum beat from one record, the string arrangement from another record, the vocal refrain from a third record, and the rhythm track from a fourth record. They then put them together on one track and rap to this new music.

Another musical technique involves discarding the words from previously released records and using the complete music track. For instance, M.C. Hammer's hit record "Can't Touch This" used the music from a 1981 song released by Rick James called "Super Freak."

Sometimes rappers also compose their own music or use a combination of original music and sampled music.

Some people criticize the rappers' constant use of other people's music. However, the different musical techniques actually give rappers freedom in creating exciting new effects—and at a very low cost.

Where Did Rap Begin?

Rap music began in the African American discos of New York City. Mel Quinn's on 42nd Street and Club 371 in the Bronx were hotbeds of early rap. In these clubs, a young man from Harlem who called himself D.J. Hollywood played records on the weekends. At this time, African American club disc jockeys often talked to their audiences in a jive style that had been around since the 1940s.

Hollywood created a more complicated, high-energy style of talking to his audiences that used rhyme. His audiences loved this style, and his reputation grew quickly by word of mouth. Tapes of his routines began to be heard around the city. Others in the area began to copy Hollywood's style. He seemed to speak directly to his African American audience.

It was Grandmaster Flash, whose real name is Joseph Saddler, who helped to bring a new sophistication to rap. As a kid, Saddler loved music—but records frustrated him. Rather than listening to them all the way through, Saddler would pick out the best parts and imagine how they would sound together.

Meeting Individual Needs: Ask students to choose a statement of fact from this section and rewrite it as a statement of opinion, using words that show they are making a judgment.

ESL/LEP: Help students clarify the meaning of the word *hotbeds*.

Additional Skills: This section on the history of rap music is also appropriate for teaching sequence (see ATE page 98).

Response Clue: Have students read this paragraph and the next and then give details that tell about Grandmaster Flash's contributions to rap music.

By his mid-teens, Saddler had created his own records by plugging two turntables into the same speaker. He would then switch constantly from one record to the other. For example, he might play a 10-second bass line from a James Brown record, a 15-second explosion from a Chic record, and so on, back and forth between the two records. This was the beginning of sampling.

Rap, however, remained an underground phenomenon until 1979. That summer, Sylvia and Joe Robinson, a husband-and-wife team who owned an eight-year-old record company called All Platinum, heard three boys rapping to music in a New York City park.

"Something about that sound hit me," Sylvia Robinson said. "I thought they were fantastic." Sylvia and Joe recruited the three youngsters, named them the Sugar Hill Gang, and recorded "Rapper's Delight." More than two million copies of the record sold in the United States. It was on Top Ten music charts in several countries. The success of "Rapper's Delight" opened the doors for rap—but the doors opened slowly.

Summarizing: Have students stop at this heading and summarize the main historical developments in the history of rap.

When Did Rap Really Take Off?

Despite the success of "Rapper's Delight," rap music did not quickly gain wide acceptance. Many listeners simply could not adjust to music that was spoken instead of sung. Many music critics dismissed rap as a musical fad that would eventually disappear. Others thought the music was noisy and crude—an attack on the middle class. Major record companies refused to record the artists. Many radio stations refused to play rap records.

It wasn't until 1982, when Grandmaster Flash and the Furious Five released a record called "The Message," that rap began to be taken seriously. "The Message," a stark tale of loneliness in the inner city, was hailed by the *Los Angeles Times*, *The New York Times*, and a number of important music publications as the best record of the year.

It was then that two brothers, Joseph and Russell Simmons, began to put rap on the map. Russell produced live rap shows around New York City. Eventually, he began managing such popular acts as Kurtis Blow and L.L. Cool J. Today, he runs Def Jam Records and Rush Management. These companies record and represent dozens of rap artists.

Russell's brother Joseph and two other friends formed a group called Run-DMC. While in college, Russell wrote the song that became another early rap classic, "It's Like That." It pushed Run-DMC into the forefront of rap.

Run-DMC reached a wider audience than previous rap acts had. For example, the group's songs appealed to whites, who had mostly ignored rap before. Consequently, the group sold millions of records and performed worldwide to sold-out audiences.

The group also adopted a catchy, outlaw image. Members wore black hats and clothing. Their trademark was untied sneakers. Run-DMC didn't want to make people think they were gangsters. They just thought they looked cool.

The Beastie Boys, a group of white rappers, made an even stronger move into the mainstream with their album *Licensed to Ill*. It combined several styles—punk, rap, and heavy metal. Through this album, many more teens became familiar with rap music. And people began to see how much profit could be made from rap music.

Influenced by these successes, dozens of other rap artists formed in the early to mid-1980s—Bizmarkie, the Fat Boys, Doug E. Fresh, Slick Rick, Whodini, L.L. Cool J, and Stetsasonic. Because major record labels continued to balk at recording rap artists, record stores became the showcases of new rap-oriented record labels. Among them were Delicious Vinyl, Ruthless Records, Select and Cold Chillin', and Def Jam.

What Are Some Forms of Rap?

In the mid-1980s, as rap music grew, it began to take on various forms. There were female-only rap groups like Salt 'n' Pepa, Queen Latifah, and M.C. Lyte. There was a new wave of "wholesome rappers." One example was D.J. Jazzy Jeff & the Fresh Prince, a clean-cut duo who scored success with "Parents Just Don't Understand."

Also emerging during the latter part of the 1980s were rap artists who emphasized pride in African American culture. Most notable were Public Enemy and Boogie Down Productions.

In the 1990s, a controversial movement in rap took off—gangster rap. It was launched in 1987 by a Compton, California, group called N.W.A. The group's records featured fires and gunshots as backdrops to their brutal tales of drug deals, gangs, and run-ins with the police. The group's first album, *Straight Outta Compton*, sold 500,000 copies in just six weeks. N.W.A. was followed by such groups as the Geto Boys, Gangstarr, Ice Cube, and Dr. Dre.

Response Clue: Ask students if the last sentence in the first paragraph on this page is a statement of fact, a statement of opinion, or a statement of fact that includes an opinion. Then ask: "How could you prove the statement to be true? What word in the sentence signals someone's opinion?"

Writing Process: Students may want to work in small groups to write their own rap songs.

Response Clue: Have students state a main idea from this section and give details that support it. Students may want to use a chart like the one on the **Introducing** page to organize their ideas.

Response Clue: Ask students to give their opinions about gangster rap. They may enjoy holding a mini-debate on the issue.

Response Clue: Ask students to state the main idea of this excerpt from *The New York Times*.

Response Clue: Ask students to describe Ice Cube's opinion about rap and violence.

Response Clue: Ask students to list details that support the first sentence in this paragraph.

Gangster rap is criticized widely because of its foul language, put-downs of women, and promotion of violence. It has been labeled "dangerous" because of events like those described below by Paul Delaney in an October 1993 issue of *The New York Times*:

The danger of [the gangster rappers'] message was clear this summer in the so-called whirlpooling trend in New York, when groups of teen-age boys, chanting rap lyrics, surrounded and . . . assaulted several girls at public swimming pools.

Ice Cube, one of the leading gangster rappers, disagrees with linking rap to violence:

People say our music inspires violence or whatever, but there has been violence since the beginning of time. . . . I like my records to wake people up, make them think . . . see something in a new way.

Dr. John Oliver, a professor at Cal State Long Beach's School of Social Work, sees rap in another way. He connects rap musicians with the 1960s soul artists, whose themes were based on African American pride:

The rappers have gone back to the ways of Sly and the Family Stone or Curtis Mayfield or Donny Hathaway, who spoke about social conditions. They are not only rallying the young rap audience into doing something actively about social problems, but also expressing black attitudes to the larger communities.

What's Ahead for Rap?

Rap continues to grow and change. Most recently, many rappers, such as Guru, Digable Planets, and Free Style, have begun to base their music around jazz instead of the funky beats of rhythm and blues. In the Latino community, "raperos" like Gerardo and Naomi have emerged.

And rap continues to be highly successful. Just how much more it will grow is unclear, but one thing seems certain: Despite all of the early predictions that rap was just a passing fad, it appears that its influence is here to stay.

If you are working on

Lesson 7 | Lesson 8

page 73 | page 75

Reviewing *Main Ideas and Details*

A. Read the article "Rap Music: What's It All About?" on pages 68-72. Underline the writer's main ideas. In the margins, note details that give more information about each main idea. Then choose one main idea you have identified along with its supporting details and complete the chart below.

Reviewing the Strategy: To complete the graphic organizer, have students write the main idea they have selected in the center of the chart and each supporting detail on the spokes.

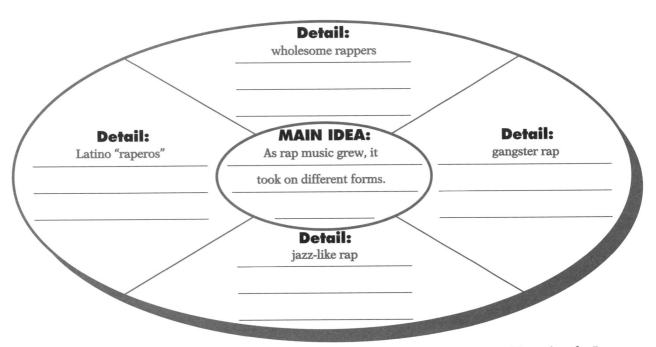

Detail:
wholesome rappers

Detail:
Latino "raperos"

MAIN IDEA:
As rap music grew, it took on different forms.

Detail:
gangster rap

Detail:
jazz-like rap

B. Write a paragraph telling about one of the author's main ideas in the article about rap music. Include some details from the article that give more information about the major point the author is making.

Student answers should discuss one of the article's main ideas and include supporting

details from the text.

Managing the Lesson: Answers on the chart are suggestions. Students may find other main ideas, such as *Rap Music began in the African American discos of New York City*, as they read the article.

Conferencing: For part B, have students work with a peer to identify the main idea and details in each other's response.

Assessing Cooperative Work: Note the degree to which group members listen to each other, contribute to the discussion, and add relevant information.

Testing **Main Ideas and Details**

A. The paragraph below is based on the rap music article on pages 68-72. Fill in each blank with the best word from the left-hand column that completes each supporting detail.

Test-Taking Hints: Suggest that students read the paragraph before they fill in the blanks. Prereading will give them clues to help them choose the best answers.

1. radio
   rock
   "Rapper's
   Delight"

2. D. J.
   Hollywood
   underground
   concerts

3. M.C. Lyte
   *The New
   York Times*
   social
   conditions

4. female-only
   rhythm and
   blues
   teenage

    Rap is one of today's hottest musical forms. It seems to be as popular as the blues, jazz, and _____rock_____, to
(1)
name a few other popular styles of music. You can hear rap music on radio, in _____concerts_____, and on television.
(2)
    Rap music has its share of outstanding performers. People like Grandmaster Flash, _____M. C. Light_____ and L.L.
(3)
Cool J may one day be in the "Rap Music Hall of Fame."

    There are various kinds of rap music, including _____female-only_____ groups, artists who emphasize pride in
(4)
African-American culture, and gangster rap.

B. Now list the three main ideas in the paragraph.

The three main ideas in the paragraph are: Rap is one of today's hot musical forms;

rap has its share of outstanding performers; and there are various kinds of rap music.

_____

_____

_____

_____

_____

_____

_____

_____

_____

_____

**To begin
Lesson 8**

↓

**page
60**

Reviewing *Fact and Opinion*

A. Reread the article about rap music on pages 68-72. As you read, identify statements of fact and statements of opinion. Note them in the margins. Identify three statements of fact or opinion to complete the diagram below.

Reviewing the Strategy: Explain that statements should be written in the left-hand columns, designations of fact or opinion in the middle columns, and responses in the right-hand columns.

Statement	Is It Fact or Opinion?	Reader's Response to Statement
Statement 1: Sales of rap records total in the hundreds of millions of dollars.	fact	Rap music is more popular than I realized.
Statement 2: Gangster rap is criticized widely . . .	opinion	This may or may not be true, depending on who you talk to.
Statement 3: The term *rap* originated as African American street slang for the word *talk*.	fact	Language changes all the time.

B. On the lines below, write a paragraph that describes your favorite kind of music. When you are finished, circle the facts that you included and underline your opinions.

Student writing should describe a favorite type of music and should include facts and

opinions that explain their choice. Make sure students have circled and

underlined correctly.

Managing the Lesson: Answers on the chart are suggestions. Students may find other statements of fact or opinion, such as *Rap, however, remained an underground phenomenon until 1979*, as they read the article.

Testing Fact and Opinion

A. The paragraph below is based on the article "Rap Music: What's It All About?" on pages 68-72. Fill in each blank with the best word or words from the lists provided.

1. believes
    proves
    disproves

2. important
    false
    true

3. fact
    opinion
    idea

4. criticize
    like
    know

5. research
    defend
    disapprove
    of

The writer _____believes_____ that rap music is here to
(1)
stay—a solid part of the music scene. It is certainly

_____true_____ that rap records sell very well. It's also a
(2)

_____fact_____ that groups like the Sugar Hill Gang and
(3)

Run DMC have sold millions of records. Some people

_____criticize_____ rap music because they think it is crude and
(4)

promotes violence. Other people _____defend_____ rap
(5)

because it addresses social problems.

B. What do you think of rap music? Write a paragraph that explains your position to your readers. Use signal words that show when you are stating your opinions.

Student writing should use facts and opinions to support their position on rap music.

Make sure students have used signal words in their paragraphs.

_____

_____

_____

_____

_____

_____

_____

_____

_____

_____

_____

_____

Unit FIVE

BECOMING AN ACTIVE READER

Good readers are strategic readers. They adjust their goals to fit the texts they are reading. For example, they approach **encyclopedia entries**, or articles, with a set of questions.

Using Skills and Strategies

Asking questions before and after reading an **encyclopedia entry** helps you to organize and remember information efficiently. Before starting to read, ask: How much do I already know about the topic? What do I need to learn? After reading, ask: What new information have I learned?

Another way to organize information is to **classify key words** into groups, or categories. You might ask: What do the words in this paragraph have in common? What other words also belong in the same category? Using this technique will help you understand new words and increase your vocabulary.

In this unit, **reading an encyclopedia entry** and **classifying words** will help you become a strategic reader.

Reading Encyclopedia Entries

When you want to learn more about a topic, look it up in an encyclopedia. Listed in alphabetical order, entries can be found on just about anything—from *Africa* under "A" to *Zunis* under "Z." To find information in long encyclopedia articles, look for subheadings that interest you.

Responding to Encyclopedia Entries

Good readers respond to encyclopedia articles by keeping track of new information as they read. It is helpful to write down what you learn as you read "Kwanzaa" and "Diego Rivera." Your notes will help you recall information that you have learned with your classmates.

Unit Enrichment: Have students use information from the encyclopedia entries to create posters or murals that show important facts about Kwanzaa or Diego Rivera.

Reading an Encyclopedia Entry

| *Lesson 9* | Introducing *page 78* | Practicing *page 79* | Applying *page 80* | Reviewing *page 93* | Testing *page 94* |

Introducing Strategies

Good readers expect to find certain information on a topic when **reading an encyclopedia entry.** They expect to find names of key people and places, events and dates, and other facts. Sometimes the entry is organized in sections under subheadings. Before reading, good readers ask themselves questions about the topic based on what they already know and what they want to find out. To find answers, readers skim the subheadings in bold type. They also look for maps, charts, graphs, or pictures. Then, as they read, they keep notes on what they learn.

The chart below shows how readers ask questions as they read an encyclopedia entry.

What do I already know about the topic?	**What do I want to know?**	**What have I learned from reading the entry?**

Reading the Encyclopedia Entry

Read the encyclopedia entry for "Kwanzaa" and the sidenotes on pages 84-85. These notes show how one good reader asked questions and responded to the information in the entry. After reading, answer the questions below.

1. Before reading the entry, how did the reader know what kinds of information the article contained?

The reader skimmed the subheads to find out what information the entry contained.

_____

2. List some things that the reader wanted to find out about Kwanzaa.

The reader wanted to know how Kwanzaa originated, what the symbols of the

holiday mean, and whether Kwanzaa is similar to or different from holidays the

reader celebrates.

Lesson Objective: To use the strategy of asking questions before, during, and after reading with the encyclopedia entries "Kwanzaa" and "Diego Rivera."

Modeling the Strategy: Using an actual encyclopedia article, model the skill of asking what do I know, what do I want to know, and what have I learned. Use the diagram and refer to subheads in your article as you read. Use the Reproducible Activity Master on page T15 of the ATE to help students apply the strategy to "Kwanzaa."

ESL/LEP: Make available a display of Kwanzaa symbols: an ear of corn, a basket of fruits and vegetables, a *kinara*, and a unity cup. Ask students to tell the meaning of each symbol after they have read "Kwanzaa."

Managing the Lesson: Remind students to carefully read the sidenotes on pages 84-85 and use them to answer items 1 and 2. The sidenotes model the skill of asking questions while reading encyclopedia entries.

Practicing **Reading an Encyclopedia Entry**

A. The incomplete statements below are based on the encyclopedia entry "Kwanzaa." Circle the letter in front of the word or words that best complete each statement. Then, on the lines provided, give some details that explain why you selected that answer.

1. A reader of this entry would not expect to learn about
   a. Kwanzaa in the year 2010.
   b. the origin of Kwanzaa.
   c. the Seven Principles of Kwanzaa.
   d. the meaning of the word *Kwanzaa*.

   Students should recognize that the year 2010 is in the future and encyclopedia entries

   only describe what already has happened.

2. By reading the entry, a reader would have learned that one reason Kwanzaa was created was to
   a. honor Dr. Martin Luther King, Jr.
   b. celebrate the heritage of African Americans.
   c. commemorate the Civil War.
   d. raise money for worthy causes.

   Students may explain their answer by citing the reasons Dr. Karenga developed

   Kwanzaa or by mentioning information in the writer's opening paragraph.

3. To help the reader quickly identify the holiday symbols of Kwanzaa, the entry includes
   a. dates.
   b. a bibliography.
   c. a photograph.
   d. subheadings.

   Students may note that looking at the photograph helped them identify the symbols.

B. Choose a subject you know a lot about. Write some subheadings you would include in an encyclopedia entry about the subject. Describe a photograph for the entry.

   Accept all reasonable responses that show students understand the kinds of

   information contained in an encyclopedia entry.

Purpose: The purpose of the **Practicing** page is to help students practice the skill of reading an encyclopedia entry. Items reflect the questioning strategy presented on the **Introducing** page.

Peer Sharing: Have students complete Section A independently, then work with a partner to compare answers. Encourage students to make sure their partners provide reasons to support their answers.

Writing Process: Students may want to use their subheadings and photograph description to write a section of an encyclopedia entry.

Applying the Skill to Other Media: Remind students that they can supplement what they learn about a topic in an encyclopedia by reading one of the books suggested at the end of an entry or by finding magazine articles or television shows about the topic. Ask students where they could find additional information about basketball.

ESL/LEP: Show students photographs from magazines or newspapers of modern basketball games. Have students compare the pictures to the description in the entry. Ask them to explain how basketball has changed.

Cooperative Learning: Have students complete the page in groups of three. Make sure that everyone in the group has a chance to contribute his or her ideas. Have groups present their answers to the class.

Applying **Reading an Encyclopedia Entry**

Read the title and subtitle of the section from an encyclopedia entry below and complete items 1 and 2. After you read the excerpt, complete item 3.

BASKETBALL
History of the Game

In 1891, a physical education instructor at a school in Springfield, Massachusetts, invented the game of basketball. The instructor, James A. Naismith, was asked to create a team sport that could be played indoors during the winter. The first basketball game was played in December 1891, using a soccer ball. Two wooden peach baskets attached to the gymnasium's railing 10 feet above the floor served as the goals.

Two years later, metal hoops with nets replaced the peach baskets. In 1894, backboards were added and larger balls were used to play the game.

1. List some things you already know about the history of basketball.

Accept all appropriate answers that pertain to the history of basketball.

_____

_____

_____

2. What would you like to know about the history of basketball? List some questions.

Accept all questions that show what else students might like to learn.

_____

_____

_____

3. What new information did you learn by reading the excerpt?

Accept any details from the passage, such as the name of the game's inventor, the

date of the first game, and the use of peach baskets.

_____

_____

_____

To review
page
93

Classifying Words

| **Lesson 10** | Introducing *page 81* | Practicing *page 82* | Applying *page 83* | Reviewing *page 95* | Testing *page 96* |

Introducing Strategies

Grouping vocabulary words into categories is called **classifying.** One way good readers do this is to think about the categories, or groups, to which key words belong. Readers also think about other words or word groups that can be added to each category. For example, they may read the words *holiday* and *food* in an article. Then they may think of words that name those foods from a special holiday. Classifying words while reading is a way of developing your vocabulary.

The diagram below shows one way to classify key words while reading.

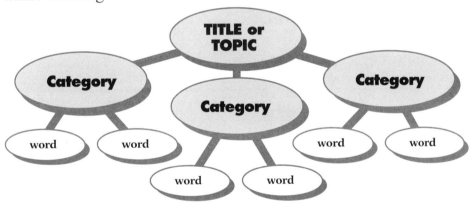

Reading the Encyclopedia Entry

Reread the encyclopedia entry for Kwanzaa on pages 84-87. As you read, circle some key words that name categories and underline words that fit into each category. Then use the words to respond to the items below.

1. List some categories that you circled as you read.

Students might list categories such as the Seven Principles of Kwanzaa, symbols,

rituals, clothing, etc.

2. Choose one of the categories that you listed in #1. Then list the words you underlined that belong in that category.

Responses will depend on the category chosen, but should correspond to words in

the text that belong in the category.

Lesson Objective: To learn how to classify key words into categories by using a clustering strategy when reading the encyclopedia entries "Kwanzaa" and "Diego Rivera."

Oral Language: Engage students in a discussion of classification by asking them to group classroom objects under categories such as reading materials, writing materials, and furniture.

ESL/LEP: Bring to class advertisements of supermarkets and department stores from newspapers or magazines. Ask students to organize the items in the ads into categories. Have them explain why each item fits into a particular category.

Modeling the Strategy: Read aloud a passage from students' classroom texts to model classifying words. Refer to the parts of the cluster diagram. Use the Reproducible Activity Master on page T15 of the ATE to help students apply the strategy to "Kwanzaa."

Managing the Lesson: Remind students to use the words they circled and underlined to complete items 1 and 2.

Practicing Classifying Words

Purpose: The purpose of the **Practicing** page is to give students practice in classifying words. Questions reflect the classification strategy illustrated in the word map on the **Introducing** page.

Peer Sharing: Have pairs of students complete Section A together. Both partners should be able to explain their responses.

A. Below are incomplete statements based on the encyclopedia entry about Kwanzaa. Circle the letter in front of the word or phrase that best completes each statement. Then, write the reason for your choice.

1. The first three of the Seven Principles of Kwanzaa are *umoja* (unity), _____, and *ujamaa* (cooperative economics).
   a. *kujichagulia* (self-determination)
   b. *mazao* (food)
   c. *karamu* (feast)

   Only self-determination belongs in the category of the Seven Principles.

2. A *Mkeka* (straw mat), a *kinara* (candle holder), and _____ can be found on tables in homes where Kwanzaa is celebrated.
   a. *vibunzi* (ears of corn)
   b. *nia* (purpose)
   c. *Harambee!* (Together!)

   Students may note that a *Mkeka*, a *kinara*, and *vibunzi* are all symbols of Kwanzaa.

3. *Lappas, dashikis,* and *kofis* are examples of _____, which are worn during Kwanzaa.
   a. horns of plenty
   b. colorful scarves
   c. traditional African clothing

   Lappas, dashikis, and *kofis* are all items of traditional African clothing.

Conferencing: Have students conference with a peer to share their chosen categories and the words that belong in them.

ESL/LEP: If students have difficulty understanding the process of classification, ask them to identify a holiday they celebrate. Then, ask them to list the foods they eat or the clothing they wear and circle the category name.

B. Write a paragraph about a holiday you like to celebrate. Choose one category, such as *food* or *symbols*, related to that holiday to write about. In your paragraph, use as many words as you can think of that belong in that category.

Accept all responses that show students understand the difference between categories

and the words that belong in a category.

_____

_____

_____

_____

_____

Applying *Classifying Words*

Read the encyclopedia excerpt below. After you read the excerpt, complete the items that follow.

BIRDS
Building a Nest

Most—but by no means all—birds build their own nests using natural materials such as grass, twigs, leaves, and mud. The female does most of the work, although the male may supply some of the building materials. Nests range from simple saucer-shaped structures to complex communal nests. Nests can be as small as a hummingbird's, which can measure as little as an inch, or as large as an osprey's nest, which can reach a width of 6 feet.

Some birds do not build their own nests. For example, starlings often use the nests of other birds after scaring them off. Most falcons lay their eggs on the bare ground. Other birds, such as bluebirds, wrens, and house sparrows, lay their eggs in hollow trees, holes in the ground, abandoned nests of other birds, or man-made bird houses.

1. List some words in the entry that name categories.

Answers may include natural materials, nest sizes, and birds that do not build their

own nests.

2. Choose one category and write words from the passage or words of your own that fit that category.

Responses will depend on the category chosen, but the words should be appropriate

to that category.

3. Now make a category listing various types of homes used by other animals. Reorder your list from the smallest home to the largest.

Under the category "types of homes used by other animals," students might list

examples such as rabbit holes, beehives, bear caves. Check that students' lists are

in proper order.

Applying the Skill to Other Disciplines: Have students show how they use the skill of classification in their physical education, music, and art classes.

Individualized Learning: Have students complete the page independently. They may want to create a word cluster to categorize information from the passage.

ESL/LEP: Encourage students to find pictures of different kinds of bird nests in library books. Students can categorize the pictures according to the types of nests mentioned in the article.

To review
page 95

For more than 20 years, Naurice Roberts has focused on writing literature for young people. She is often asked to give motivational speeches that emphasize self-esteem and develop pride in her African American heritage. For these reasons, Kwanzaa is a celebration she especially likes to promote.

KWANZAA

by Naurice Roberts

The notes in the margin on pages 84 and 85 show one reader's thoughts while reading an encyclopedia entry. Notice that the sidenotes reflect what the reader already knows, hopes to find out, and then actually learns.

This first paragraph tells in a general way what Kwanzaa is. I'll skim the section headings to find out what specific information is given about Kwanzaa.

▶ KWANZAA is an African American holiday. The celebration combines the unique cultural, social, and historical experiences of Africans and African Americans. It is considered the only such holiday for African Americans in the United States. However, it is not an official or legal holiday.

The word *Kwanzaa* comes from the Swahili phrase *Matunde ya Kwanza*, which means "first fruits." (Swahili is one of many African languages. Many Swahili words are used in the celebration of Kwanzaa.) The second "a" was added at the end of the word *Kwanza* to distinguish the African American word from the African word.

In farming regions of Africa, traditional villages celebrated the "first fruits" of the harvest. They did this because they believed the earth gave them their food. Therefore, Africans regularly showed thanks for what the earth produced.

Making Predictions: Ask students to predict what the entry will be about after skimming the title, headnote, and first paragraph.

Unlike the Africans from whom they are descended, African Americans today typically are not farmers but live in or near cities. Thus, Kwanzaa in the United States celebrates a gathering or reunion of family and friends in the African tradition.

ESL/LEP: Explain to students the practice of using italics for non-English words and parentheses for explanatory information or English translations.

Origin

I'm curious about how Kwanzaa originated. This section will probably tell me.

▶ Kwanzaa was created in 1965 by ⟨Dr. Maulana⟩ ⟨Karenga⟩, a political scientist in California. He thought African Americans should come together in the spirit of their ancestors and celebrate themselves. So, he developed a holiday which would focus on the many accomplishments and achievements of African Americans. Dr. Karenga felt the celebration of Kwanzaa would provide identity, purpose, and direction for the African American community.

Response Clue: Students may have circled the name *Dr. Maulana Karenga* and underlined words that belong in that topic category.

Nguzo Saba, the Seven Principles

The basis or foundation of Kwanzaa is a special value

system called the *nguzo saba*, or the Seven Principles. These principles offer African Americans direction and guidance, not only as individuals, but also collectively as a community.

The Seven Principles are: *umoja* (unity), *kujichagulia* (self-determination), *ujima* (collective work and responsibility), *ujamaa* (cooperative economics), *nia* (purpose), *kuumba* (creativity), and *imani* (faith). These principles are studied and practiced in the order they are listed. That is, each of the seven days of the celebration of Kwanzaa has one principle as its theme.

The Symbols

Kwanzaa, like many other holidays, has tremendous symbolism built into the celebration. Interpretation and understanding of the symbolism are key.

The symbols of Kwanzaa appear on a table in the home in which the holiday is celebrated. *Mkeka* (the straw mat covering the table) is the symbol of tradition and history. *Mazao* (food, or crops—usually a basket filled with fruits and vegetables) exemplifies the historical roots of the holiday and the results of collective community work. *Kinara* (a candle holder for seven candles) represent the family's ancestors, whereas *vibunzi* (ears of corn) symbolize the children. Families are encouraged to have an ear of corn for each child in the household. The *kikombe cha umoja* (unity cup) symbolizes the first principle—*umoja,* or unity.

The seven candles, called the *mishumaa saba*, placed in the *kinara* represent the Seven Principles. The candles are black, red, and green. Black depicts African Americans in unity. Red represents the blood of the ancestors. Green is for the land of Africa and the hope of young people. The black candle is placed in the center of the *kinara*. Since it stands for the first principle, it is lit first. Three red candles are placed to the left of the black candle and three green candles to the right. A red or green candle is lit on the second day and subsequent days, alternately, until all candles are lit.

Dates

Kwanzaa begins the day after Christmas, December 26, and continues for seven days through January 1. Each day focuses on one of the Seven Principles. For instance, on December 26, the first day of Kwanzaa, the emphasis is on *umoja* (unity), the first principle. On January 1, the seventh or final day of the holiday, *imani* (faith), the last principle, is featured.

Principles are like rules or unwritten laws to live by. The seven principles seem to focus on working together. But I don't know what *cooperative economics* means.

Clarification: You may wish to have students reread this section to help them clarify the meaning of the Seven Principles.

Cultural Awareness: Have students describe symbols used in their own culture's celebrations.

I wonder if the symbols of Kwanzaa are like the symbols of Thanksgiving.

Response Clue: In this paragraph, students may have circled the word *symbols* and underlined words that belong in that category.

Lighting candles is similar to what I do at Hanukkah! How is the Kwanzaa ceremony different?

Write your own sidenotes as you read the rest of the article. In your notes, focus on things you already know, things you want to know more about, and any new information you learn.

Summarizing: Have students stop reading at this point and summarize the main ideas of the entry. Students should include information about the origins of Kwanzaa, its Seven Principles, and its symbols.

Cooperative Learning: Divide the class into small groups. Have each group create an illustrated calendar celebrating Kwanzaa. Tell students to make a box for each day of Kwanzaa. They should make drawings and write explanations for the principles that are observed on each day. Students may also include the ceremonies they have read about in this entry.

Response Clue: Students may have circled the word *rituals*. Have students tell which words they underlined for that category.

Response Clue: Students may have noted some information in this paragraph that they had wanted to find out about Kwanzaa.

Cultural Awareness: Students who are familiar with Kwanzaa might like to describe the foods served during the *karamu*. Other students may describe similar food from their own cultures or from cultures they know about.

During the seven days, someone may ask, *"Habari gani?"* or "What's the news?" The response depends on the day. If it's day three, the reply would be *"Ujima, habari gani!"* or "Working together is the news!"

Ceremonies and Rituals

The seven days of Kwanzaa are filled with activities including ceremonies, rituals, and programs conducted and performed at schools, churches, and community centers. Many are also held in homes with participation by the entire family.

There are a number of rituals or ceremonies in the celebration of Kwanzaa. Some vary, depending on the region of the country. At dinner on the first day of Kwanzaa, the _kinara_ is brought to the table and the first candle is lit. The adults lead a _discussion_ about unity. The children are asked to give their input—their personal ideas, concepts, and views on the principle for the day. The discussion is usually lengthy. After dinner the candle is blown out. On the second day, the first candle plus another candle are lit, the principle of the day is discussed, and so the ritual continues over a seven-day period.

The _karamu_, or big feast, is celebrated on either December 31 or January 1. The entire community gathers in a special festival of rituals, discussions, music, dances, food, fun, and fellowship. After drinking from the <u>cup of unity</u>, all say *"Harambee!"* or *"Together!"*

    <u>Gifts</u> are given on January 1. Called *zawadi*, they symbolize promises or commitments the children have made and kept since the previous Kwanzaa and also the fruits of parents' work. Kwanzaa discourages commercialism and encourages imagination and creativity in gift giving.

Decorations and Attire

    Special (decorations) and clothing are also part of the Kwanzaa celebration. Prior to Kwanzaa, rooms are decorated in red, black, and green streamers and flags, called *banderas*. A <u>horn of plenty</u>, often seen during the traditional U.S. Thanksgiving holiday, is often included in Kwanzaa decor. It represents the harvest and fruits of labor.

    Other decorations include the <u>sun</u>, in all the colors it projects from sunrise to sunset—yellow, orange, and red. The sun stands for creation and growth. A yellow or red Ankh, an <u>Egyptian cross</u> with a circle on top, is displayed in windows. It symbolizes life.

    Traditional African (dress) is an important part of the spirit of the celebration, especially at the *karamu*. Women and girls wear a *lappa* or *buba*, an African dress. Men and boys wear *dashikis* or *kanzus*, which are special shirts, and small round hats called *kofis*.

    The celebration of Kwanzaa has grown tremendously since its beginning. It is estimated that millions of African Americans celebrate the holiday, with the numbers increasing as years progress.

    See also HOLIDAY.

    For further reading: Curtis, Dorothy L., *A Celebration of Kwanzaa* (Vantage 1991); Copage, Eric, *Kwanzaa: A Celebration of Culture and Cooking* (Morrow 1991); *The African American Holiday of Kwanzaa*, The University of Sankore Press, 2560 West 54th Street, Los Angeles, California 90043, (213) 299-6124.

Response Clue: In their sidenotes, students may have suggested what they learned by reading this section.

Meeting Individual Needs: If students have difficulty classifying words, refer them to this paragraph. Tell them to look for words that belong to the category of African clothing.

Student Self-Assessment: Ask students to rate themselves in the following areas on a scale of 1-4, with 1 being the least degree and 4 being the greatest degree: ability to utilize the strategy, ease in writing sidenotes, and ability to transfer skill to reading. (Make clear that student responses are for their own purposes only.)

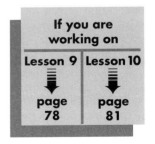

If you are working on

Lesson 9	Lesson 10
⬇	⬇
page 78	page 81

Mary Lou Nevarez Haugh sets up art shows for Latino artists in the San Francisco Bay area. Her soon-to-be-published book includes interviews with more than 100 of these California artists. Haugh has said that she loves "working with artists and learning about their lives. . . . They are the ones who motivate and inspire me."

Diego Rivera

by Mary Lou Nevarez Haugh

RIVERA, DIEGO (1886-1957) was one of the most famous and influential Mexican painters of his time. He began the tradition of Mexican mural paintings. His larger-than-life murals cover the walls of many of North America's most famous buildings. The images in his paintings reflect social and political messages and community goals. He helped create a national Mexican style of painting, reflecting Mexican history and social revolution.

Early Life and Schooling

Diego Rivera was born in Guanajuato, a town in central Mexico, on December 8, 1886. His twin brother died when the boys were one-and-a-half years old. Diego himself was very weak as a child. When he was quite young, the doctor advised his parents to send him to the country, where he would have a better chance to get strong and healthy than he would in the town.

Later, when Rivera was six years old, he moved to Mexico City with his family. It was there, at the age of eight, that he entered school for the first time. He was soon promoted to the sixth grade because he was so bright. He had learned a great deal from his father, who had been a teacher. At thirteen, Rivera entered the San Carlos School of Fine Arts in Mexico City.

Early Influences on Rivera's Art

Diego Rivera's interest in art began when he was young enough to hold pencils and crayons. He drew on nearly everything around him. His parents recognized his strong desire to draw and gave him a room of his own. They allowed him to draw on the walls, doors, and anything else in his special room. One of the first detailed images he drew was of a train. His fascination with machines continued throughout his life.

While at the San Carlos School of Fine Arts, Rivera won prizes and was offered scholarships. But as he grew older, he felt that something was missing from his education at the school of fine arts. He wanted to learn more about the natural world and about machines. He decided to study mechanical drawing. And so, he transferred to the San Carlos School of Architecture, where he studied mechanics, advanced geometry, and the laws of optics under the instruction of José Maria Velasco.

At the same time, Rivera began studying Pre-Columbian art, which was made by the native Mexicans before the arrival of Columbus. The ancient art left a deep emotional impression on Rivera. He felt that the artworks expressed joy, fear, and hope and showed what life had been like long ago.

Early Political Ideas

Rivera and many of his fellow students felt that they needed to learn new ideas about art. At the age of sixteen, Diego led an organized strike for better education. The strike turned into a riot, and Rivera was expelled from school. After the incident, he studied on his own and under the artist-engraver José Guadalupe Posada.

Then in 1906, Rivera became involved with a workers' strike in the textile mills in Orizaba. The owners of the factories that make fabric had changed their rules, making life very difficult for the workers, so the workers went on strike. President Díaz sent soldiers to Orizaba, who shot many of the workers. Other workers were arrested. Diego Rivera joined the strikers and was put into prison. This experience inspired him to work for the poor and oppressed. He is still viewed by many as a revolutionary with a paintbrush. His work often reflects his efforts to bring about change.

Time Spent in Europe

While studying on his own, Rivera met many artists and other people who had traveled extensively. They inspired Rivera to plan to study in Europe. After working and showing his art in Mexico for another year, Rivera received money from the government to study and work in Spain. Rivera was now in his early twenties.

Rivera first studied in Spain. Then he traveled to France, Belgium, and England, where he went to art galleries and met many artists. Among his artistic friends there were some very famous artists—Picasso, Derain,

Response Clue: Ask students whether they have learned any of the things they wanted to know about Rivera. If they wish, they may add more items to their list of things they want to know.

Cultural Awareness: Show students examples of Pre-Columbian art. Ask them why they think Rivera would be interested in studying such art.

Making Predictions: Ask students how they think this experience affected Rivera's artwork.

Summarizing: Suggest that students stop reading here and summarize Rivera's life up to this point.

Response Clue: Ask students which words in this paragraph belong in the category of famous artists.

ESL/LEP: If some students have difficulty understanding this paragraph, they might benefit from seeing pictures of Picasso's Cubist paintings.

Response Clues: For the category "artistic styles," students may have underlined *Cubist movement*, *fresco painting*, and *murals*, on page 91.

Cultural Awareness: Encourage students to describe people from their own cultures who have made important contributions to art, music, or literature.

Response Clue: Students may have noted what they have learned about the style of Rivera's art.

Braque, Klee, Gris, and Modigliani. Rivera was well liked, and he met many sculptors and poets, too. He earned money by sending his paintings back to Mexico, where they were bought by collectors.

In 1910, he returned to Mexico when Governor Dehesa supported a solo exhibit of Rivera's work. The show was a big success for Rivera. But he soon became involved in a revolt against President Díaz and joined Zapata's revolutionary forces. After six months Rivera went back to Europe.

From 1913 to 1917, he painted and experimented with the Cubist style. Picasso, who was famous for his Cubist paintings, influenced Rivera. Cubism is an abstract style of painting that uses geometric shapes and depicts several views of an object at the same time. Although influenced by the Cubist movement, Rivera did not totally adopt the style of the group. Instead, he incorporated its ideas into his own style, which had distinctly recognizable images. In 1921, he was encouraged by the new president of Mexico to return to his homeland where he worked with David Alfaro Siqueiros to develop a Mexican national art movement.

Rivera's Success as an Artist

During the 1920s and 1930s, Rivera became an important force in Mexico's artistic development. He brought back old artistic styles but found new ways of using materials. He also used old ways of using materials to create new styles. Most importantly, he contributed to the revival of fresco painting in Mexico and the United States. Frescoes are paintings made on wet plaster. When the plaster dries, the painting becomes part of the wall or ceiling. Rivera's colors were rich, bright, deep, and harmonious. He showed the beauty of the Mexican people in the markets, the fields, the factories, and at festivals.

Rivera believed in giving messages against injustice through his art. He focused on revolutions and events with social and political importance. The War of Independence and the Revolution of 1910 were common subjects of his paintings. His art had, and still has, direct popular appeal. He included people from all the ethnic groups that make up the rich heritage of the Mexican people. His paintings reflect his vision of modern-day Mexican society and his sympathy for the workers. Some of his murals show workers and machines, a theme developed during his youth.

In the early 1930s Rivera became influential in the United States as well. He was invited to paint frescoes in San Francisco, Detroit, and New York. He also traveled extensively in Germany, the Soviet Union, and the United States. At the Art Institute in Detroit, Michigan, Rivera painted murals of factories and machines, reflecting his admiration for workers and his love of machines. He showed the events of the workers' day. He visited factories and made hundreds of sketches to produce 27 panels with themes of industrial life. He believed that men and machines were more important than legendary heroes. He painted murals of the steel industry, the automobile, and various kinds of factories.

Rivera believed he knew the worker because he viewed himself as one. He had never worked in an automobile factory, but he had worked hard as an artist. He felt he understood the struggle of the worker. That struggle is what he tried to portray in the murals he created in Detroit.

Controversy About His Art

Diego Rivera chose controversial topics for his artworks. As a result, many people were angered by what they saw in his murals. For example, the industrial murals he created in Detroit were fiercely criticized. Some people did not consider the murals beautiful. Other critics objected to the glorification of machines in the artworks. At the time, many people thought that industry treated workers like machines instead of like human beings. Still others attacked the murals for not showing the great things that industry has done for the people.

Some people wanted to destroy these paintings. Rivera was distressed when he heard of the plans to get rid of them. However, as a painter, he felt making his art was as necessary as breathing. He was not merely a man

Cooperative Learning: On a world map, have small groups of students locate the cities, countries, and continents to which Rivera traveled.

Making Predictions: Have students read this subheading and then predict what was controversial about Rivera's art.

Additional Skills: This section can also be used for teaching fact and opinion (see ATE page 60).

painting, but a man developing himself by the act of producing art. Just as a tree produces flowers and fruit and loses this bounty each year, he too would continue with his art, and not mourn over his loss. In the end, the paintings were not destroyed and are still very popular in the museum collection.

The murals *Portrait of America,* created for the lobby of the RCA Building in Rockefeller Center, were even more controversial and caused many problems for Rivera. He had included in the mural a portrait of Lenin, a Communist revolutionary leader in the Soviet Union. At the time, people in the United States feared communism. As a result, Rivera was asked by the Rockefellers to remove the portrait, but he refused. He was paid for his work and ordered to leave. Within an hour of his departure, carpenters had covered the murals. Rivera reproduced the murals in the Palace of Fine Arts in Mexico City with the new title *Man at the Crossroads, Looking with Uncertainty but with Hope to a Better World.*

Diego Rivera died on November 25, 1957, three years after the death of his wife Frida Kahlo Rivera, who was also a talented artist. His 71 years of life were filled with the struggle and development of his career as an artist. His art speaks of his great creativity and his immense power with the paintbrush.

Great artists are people with strong ideas about life and death and good and evil. Rivera was a political man as well as an artist, and he had strong ideas that he expressed through his art. He was politically involved and wrote for the newspaper of the Communist Party of Mexico. He also helped form a union of technical workers, painters, and sculptors. He worked against the Nazis before World War II. During José Vasconcelos's administration as the Minister of Education, Rivera's murals appeared in many places in Mexico. His greatest art appears in the Ministry of Education Building in Mexico City, the Palace of Cortes in Cuernavaca, and the National Palace in Mexico City.

See also PAINTING and MURAL.

Bibliography

- Helm, MacKinley. *Modern Mexican Painters, Rivera, Orozco, Siqueros, and Other Artists of the Social Realist School.* (Dover Publications, 1941)
- Hurlburt, Laurance P. *The Mexican Muralists in the United States.* (University of New Mexico Press, 1989)
- Rosenlum, Morris. *Heroes of Mexico.* (Fleet Press, 1969)

Reviewing Reading an Encyclopedia Entry

A. Read the encyclopedia entry "Diego Rivera" on pages 88-92. When you have finished, use the sidenotes you wrote to help you fill in the chart below.

What do I already know about Diego Rivera?	What do I want to know?	What have I learned from reading the entry?
Students responses will vary. Some students may know that Rivera is a well-known Mexican artist.	Student responses may include where Rivera was born, what kinds of art he created, where he studied.	Students responses will vary, but may include why Rivera was a controversial artist, where his artwork can be seen.

B. Write a paragraph that explains what else you would like to know about Diego Rivera and why you think that information would be interesting or important.

Accept all appropriate responses. Students' writing should reflect information not

included in the entry and should give reasons why the information would be

important or interesting.

_____

_____

_____

_____

_____

_____

_____

_____

_____

_____

Reviewing the Strategy: To complete the graphic organizer, have students refer to the sidenotes they wrote on pages 88-92. Tell students to list in the left-hand column what they knew about Rivera before reading the entry, what they wanted to learn in the middle column, and what they did learn in the right-hand column.

Writing Self-Assessment: Students might wish to evaluate their own writing on a scale of 1-4, with 1 being the least degree and 4 being the greatest degree. Have them use the following criteria: Did I answer the question? Are my ideas clearly stated?

Testing *Reading an Encyclopedia Entry*

Test-Taking Hints:
Remind students that it is important to follow directions exactly when they are taking tests. Sometimes a correct answer may not be counted if they failed to follow instructions.

Cooperative Learning:
Have students work in small groups to share their answers for Section A. They should support their choices with evidence from the review entry.

A. The statements below are based on the encyclopedia entry about Diego Rivera on pages 88-92. Put an X in front of each statement that is true.

[X] **1.** One quick way to discover what kind of information the entry contains is to skim the subheadings.

[ ] **2.** A reader would expect the entry to contain information about Mexican holidays.

[X] **3.** The opening paragraph provides general information on who Diego Rivera was and what he did.

[X] **4.** The purpose of the entry is to give the reader important biographical information about Diego Rivera and his work.

[ ] **5.** The purpose of the entry is to prove that Diego Rivera's ideas were dangerous.

[X] **6.** If readers wanted to know more about cubism, they could look in the encyclopedia under the entry words "Picasso, Pablo."

[X] **7.** One way to "see" Rivera's art is to look at the photographs that are included.

[ ] **8.** The reader would expect to learn about Rivera's early schooling under the subheading "Early Political Ideas."

B. The first sentence of an encyclopedia entry for Guion Bluford reads, "Bluford, Guion Stewart (1942-) was the first African American astronaut to travel in space." Write a paragraph that describes the kind of information you would expect to learn by reading the rest of the entry.

Paragraphs may include information such as place of birth, family, education,
_____
training to be an astronaut, and Bluford's historic space trip.
_____
_____
_____
_____
_____
_____
_____

To begin Lesson 10
page 81

Reviewing *Classifying Words*

A. Reread the encyclopedia entry "Diego Rivera" on pages 88-92. As you read, circle words that name categories and underline words that belong in each category. Choose two of the circled categories and underlined words and use them to fill in the chart below.

Reviewing the Strategy: Have students complete the cluster diagram according to the directions provided. Students might work on the cluster individually or in pairs. Then students can compare their clusters to see how many categories they came up with.

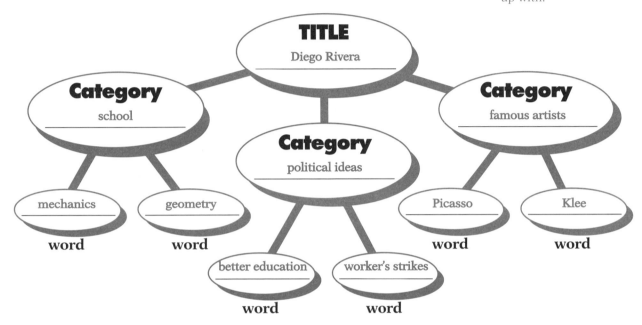

B. Write a description of a store that sells different categories of merchandise, such as a grocery store or sporting goods store. Classify words to show the kinds of merchandise in each category.

Accept any reasonable responses that show students have identified categories and

have properly classified words belonging to those categories.

Lesson Management: Answers in the cluster are suggestions. Students may find additional categories and words such as *childhood days* or *Diego's murals.*

Testing Classifying Words

A. Each incomplete statement below is based on the encyclopedia entry about Diego Rivera on pages 88-92. Fill in the oval in front of the choice that BEST completes the sentence. Then on the lines provided, explain why you selected that choice.

1. Fine arts, mechanics, geography, and optics are all examples of
   ○ careers in medicine.
   ● subjects Diego Rivera studied as a young man.
   ○ artistic movements before Diego Rivera lived.
   ○ causes of revolution.

   The words all belong in the category of school subjects.

2. Better education, workers' rights, and using his art to speak out against injustice are all
   ○ reasons for strikes in which Rivera participated.
   ● political goals Rivera felt very strongly about.
   ○ subjects of papers Rivera wrote while he was in school.
   ○ reasons why Rivera was jailed several times.

   The first, third, and last choices are not correct categories for the phrases *better education, workers' rights,* and *using his art to speak out against injustice.*

3. The words *abstract style, geometric shapes,* and *several views* all describe
   ○ mechanical drawing, which Rivera studied.
   ○ Rivera's Mexican mural paintings.
   ● Cubism, a style of painting in which Rivera was interested.
   ○ frescoes, paintings done on wet plaster.

   Student responses may refer to the details of the description of Cubism in the entry.

B. Think about a career in which you are interested. List some words in one category of words related to that career. On a separate sheet of paper, write a paragraph about the career. Use some of the words you listed in your paragraph.

Accept any reasonable responses that show students have mastered the skill of categorizing.

Unit SIX

BECOMING AN ACTIVE READER

When reading **how-to articles**, good readers often create pictures in their minds. Visualizing can help readers understand the process being described.

Using Skills and Strategies

Noticing the **sequence** in how-to articles will help you understand how the steps are related to each other. As you read, you might ask: What happened first? Then what happened? What happened last? Are several things taking place at the same time? What will happen if I reorder the steps?

Another way to understand how steps are related is to look for **causes and effects**. Try asking: What happened as a result of something earlier? Is there more than one cause? Did several things happen because of an event?

In this unit, understanding **sequence** and analyzing **cause and effect** relationships will help you become a good reader.

The How-to Article: The Writer's Voice

Every writer has a set of traditions, celebrations, special foods, music, or experiences to share with readers. Often writers share their experiences and traditions through how-to articles. This type of article can inform the reader about the writer's culture, or it can provide the reader with useful information. Look for the writer's unique voice as you read how-to articles.

Responding to How-to Articles

Good readers respond to how-to articles by keeping track of directions. Jot down the different steps as you read "How to Buy a Used Sports Car" and "How to Make Tasty, Nutritious Recipes with Beans." Your notes will help you visualize what interested you most as you share what you have learned with your classmates.

Unit Enrichment: Have students use information from the articles to stage a how-to television show about buying a used car or cooking a recipe.

Sequence

Introducing Strategies

Lesson Objective: To identify the sequence of steps in the how-to articles "How to Buy a Used Sports Car" and "How to Make Tasty, Nutritious Recipes With Beans," using signal words and prior knowledge.

ESL/LEP: Make available several comic strips from the newspaper. Ask students to describe the sequence of events in them.

Modeling the Strategy: Read aloud a passage from the students' classroom texts to model sequence. Refer to the diagram as you identify signal words and steps. Use the Reproducible Activity Master on page T16 of the ATE to help students apply the strategy to "How to Buy a Used Sports Car."

Managing the Lesson: Remind students to carefully read the sidenotes on pages 104-105 as they read the selection. The sidenotes model the skill of figuring out sequence.

One way to learn to do something is to read how-to articles. Good readers look for a **sequence** of steps in how-to articles. These steps tell readers what to do and often contain signal words such as *first, next,* and *last.* Writers may also use the words *then, finally,* and *meanwhile* to give clues to the sequence. Sometimes there are no signal words. Readers must use what they know to figure out the sequence.

The diagram below shows one way to use sequence for keeping track of details as you read a how-to article.

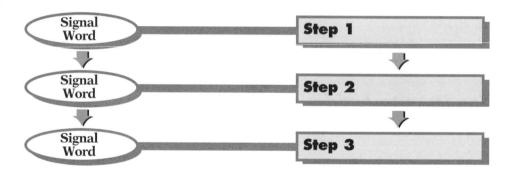

Reading the How-to Article

Read the article "How to Buy a Used Sports Car" on pages 104-109 and the sidenotes on pages 104 and 105. These notes show how one good reader paid attention to the sequence of steps in buying a used car. After reading, complete the items below.

1. List some signal words that helped the reader figure out what steps to follow during the early stages of buying a used sports car.

Signal words include *before, first, next.*

2. What is the first step the reader needs to take before buying a used sports car?

The first step is to determine how much money the reader can afford to pay.

Practicing *Sequence*

A. Each group of statements below is based on the article "How to Buy a Used Sports Car." Put the statements in the proper sequence by putting a "1" before the first step, a "2" before the second, and so on. Then list any signal words that supported your choices.

1. _3_ The next thing a buyer needs to find out is what it costs to register and insure the car.

   _1_ Before purchasing a car, a buyer needs to decide how much money is available to pay for a car.

   _4_ After subtracting all the extra costs from the available amount of money, the buyer will know how much he or she can spend on a car.

   _2_ Next, the buyer must figure out the cost of maintaining the car.

   Signal words are *before, next, next thing,* and *after.*

2. _2_ After selecting a car, the buyer should ask to take it for a test drive.

   _1_ When shopping at the used car lot, the buyer should first ask several questions about the car's condition.

   _4_ At last, the buyer can try to negotiate a price for the car with the salesperson.

   _3_ If the car performs well on the road test, the next step is a trip to the mechanic.

   Signal words are *first, after, next, at last.*

B. Write a paragraph that describes how to complete a simple task—for example, changing a tire. Use signal words to help your reader complete the task successfully.

Accept all appropriate responses that give directions in sequence and use signal
words to show the order of the steps.

Purpose: The purpose of the **Practicing** page is to help students practice the skill of sequence. Questions reflect the strategy shown in the graphic organizer on the **Introducing** page.

Peer Sharing: Have students complete Section A independently, then work with a partner to compare answers. Encourage students to make sure their partners provide reasons to support their answers.

Oral Language: Ask pairs of students to describe what they did yesterday, using signal words to show the sequence of events.

ESL/LEP: Ask volunteers to share examples of words that signal sequence in their first languages. For example. is there a word for *finally*? What is the word for *first*? Do they use other words to signal sequence?

Applying Sequence

A. Read the article below, which describes how to change the oil in a car. Then answer the questions that follow.

EVERYTHING YOU NEED TO KNOW TO CHANGE THE OIL IN A CAR

The oil in a car needs changing every 3,000 miles. This is actually an easy task to do. Before you begin, gather a container for the old oil, three or four quarts of the type of oil your car's engine requires, and a funnel. First, slide the container under the oil drain hole at the bottom of the engine and undo the drain plug. Let the old oil drain completely—this takes about half an hour—then remember to replace the drain plug. Next, find and open the oil cap on the top of your engine—it's usually marked with an arrow. Finally, pour the fresh oil into the engine (a funnel may make this easier). Above all, make sure to replace the oil cap and dispose of the used oil properly (most service stations accept used oil for recycling).

1. List the steps for changing the oil in a car.

Students should list: gather items; slide container under drain; undo plug; drain old

oil; replace plug; open oil cap; pour in fresh oil; replace cap; dispose of used oil.

2. List signal words that helped you figure out the order in which to perform the steps.

Signal words should include *before, first, then, next, finally, above all.*

B. Think of a household chore or task you usually do. Write out the steps for completing the task. Use signal words that will enable a younger brother or sister to understand the directions clearly.

Accept all appropriate responses that list steps in proper sequence and use

signal words.

To review
⇟
➜
page
117

Cause and Effect

| Lesson 12 | Introducing page 101 | Practicing page 102 | Applying page 103 | Reviewing page 119 | Testing page 120 |

Introducing Strategies

Good readers pay attention to causes and effects in how-to articles. They know that not paying attention to causes and effects can lead to unexpected results! A **cause** is the reason something happens. The **effect** is what happens as a result. Sometimes authors state causes and effects directly. Other times, readers must figure out the missing information from their own experiences. Signal words such as *therefore, consequently, because,* and *as a result* can alert you to a cause-and-effect relationship.

The diagram below is a way to think about cause-and-effect relationships while reading.

CAUSE
(the reason)

EFFECT
(the result)

Reading the How-to Article

Reread the article "How to Buy a Used Sports Car" on pages 104-109. As you read, circle words or phrases that are causes or effects, and underline any signal words. If possible, draw lines to connect causes with their effects.

1. List some of the causes and effects you identified.

Accept all responses that show that students have grasped the idea of cause and effect

relationships, such as "Eddie didn't do his homework. Therefore, he couldn't afford to

keep his car."

2. Write a signal word that alerted you to a cause-and-effect relationship. Explain the relationship.

Accept all reasonable words that denote a cause-and-effect relationship, such as

because, that's why, etc. Make sure students explain the relationship they have

identified.

Lesson Objective: To learn how to identify causes and effects through signal words and personal experience in the how-to articles "How to Buy a Used Sports Car" and "How to Make Tasty, Nutritious Recipes With Beans."

Oral Language: Ask students to discuss causes and effects they have noticed in their everyday lives. You might begin the discussion by asking, "What might cause you to change your mind about going on a picnic?"

Modeling the Strategy: Use a simple example of cause and effect to show how the diagram could be completed. For example, "Because it rained, the baseball game was cancelled." Use the Reproducible Activity Master on page T12 of the ATE to help students apply the strategy to the article "How to Buy a Used Sports Car."

Managing the Lesson: Remind students to read carefully the sidenotes on pages 104-105 as they read the selection. The sidenotes model the practice of active reading by identifying causes and effects.

Practicing **Cause and Effect**

A. The incomplete statements below are based on the article "How to Buy a Used Sports Car." Circle the letter next to the words that best complete each statement. Then, on the lines provided, tell if your answer is a cause or an effect.

1. Because Eddie didn't "do his homework,"
   a. he ran out of cash and couldn't afford to keep the car.
   b. he asked his parents to take the car away from him.
   c. he wished he had chosen a car made in the United States.
   d. he got a real bargain on the car.

   The correct answer is an effect of "not doing his homework."

2. According to the article, insurance costs for young drivers are high because
   a. young drivers can afford to pay more.
   b. all young drivers drive foreign sports cars.
   c. insurance companies favor young drivers.
   d. inexperienced drivers have more accidents.

   The correct answer is a cause of the high cost of insurance for young drivers.

3. The article suggests that a buyer test drive a used car in order to
   a. pay more than the asking price.
   b. lend money to the salesman.
   c. discover how the car handles on the road.
   d. avoid having a mechanic inspect the car.

   The correct answer is an effect of test driving a car.

B. Think of a time in your own life when you "didn't do your homework" and something unexpected happened. Write a paragraph that explains the situation.

Accept all responses that show the effects that resulted from "not doing one's homework."

Applying *Cause and Effect*

As you read the article below, think about the causes and effects of the events. Then complete the items that follow.

WHY I WILL CALL THE PLUMBER FROM NOW ON

You wouldn't think a drip under the kitchen sink would have anything to do with our kitchen wall falling down, would you? But it did. Let me tell you about it.

Last week the pipe under our kitchen sink sprang a leak. "I'll fix it," Hank said after looking at the pipe. "The joint needs tightening. Don't call the plumber." First, Hank tightened the joint. But he must have tightened it a little more than it could stand because it broke in the middle of the night. We woke up to a flooded kitchen, dining room, and living room. As a consequence, we had to call the plumber and take the morning off from work to mop up.

But flooding doesn't do a house any good. That night we noticed that the kitchen wall was water-stained. "Well, I can paint that wall again, that's easy enough," Hank observed. But the next morning we woke up to find the wet wall in a puddle on the floor. As a result, we had to call the contractor to put up a new wall. Therefore, from now on, I'm not letting Hank fix things around the house. From now on, I'm calling the plumber.

1. List the causes and effects described in the article.

Lists should include: a drip under the sink caused the kitchen wall to fall down;

because Hank tightened the joint too much, it broke during the night and the house

flooded; because the house flooded, they had to call the plumber and take the

morning off from work; when the wet wall fell down, they had to call the contractor;

because of these experiences, Hank can't fix anything around the house anymore.

2. Which signal words in the article alerted you to the cause and effect relationships?

Signal words students may list include *because, as a consequence, as a result, therefore.*

To review

page 119

Applying the Skill to Other Disciplines: Have students give examples of how they identify cause and effect relationships as they read social studies or science books.

Peer Sharing: Have students complete the page with a classmate. Both partners should contribute to the list of causes and effects in Question 1 and the list of signal words in Question 2.

ESL/LEP: Students may want to draw a cartoon of one event from the selection. Ask them to tell what caused the event to happen.

Writing Process: Students may want to write a humorous description of what happened when someone tried to fix something in their own homes.

Preteaching Vocabulary: You may wish to preteach the following words: *insurance agent, incidentals, coverage, installments, maintenance, registration.*

Making Predictions: Ask students to predict what kind of information the article will contain by reading the title and headnote.

Brian Alexander is an award-winning journalist who especially enjoys travel writing. When he's not traveling to exotic locations, Alexander can be found driving around his home base of San Diego in a practical, but sporty, two-door sedan. As this article shows, he knows that a sports car can be an expensive investment.

The sidenotes show how one reader noted the sequence of steps in buying a used sports car.

ESL/LEP: Bring to class samples from the used car section of the local paper. Ask students to look for the least expensive, the most expensive, the newest, and the oldest cars.

Response Clues: Suggested signal words are under lined. Circles and arrows show cause and effect relationships.

This part of the article is an introduction. Eddie *didn't do his homework* means he didn't do enough research. What should he have done first? The words *The First Step* in the subhead on the next page is a clue. Also, the word *Before* at the beginning of the paragraph tells me what first step I should take before I begin shopping. I need to figure out how much I can afford.

Clarification: You may want to have students reread this paragraph and list the expenses that the people waiting in line represent.

How To Buy a Used Sports Car

by Brian Alexander

The sight of Eddie Shames riding his bike to school that Monday morning really started some conversation. Ever since he had driven up in that cherry red foreign job with the chrome wheel covers, the wooden steering wheel, the five-speed overdrive and the hot attitude, Eddie had been on top of the world.

Now here he was, dressed in the leather jacket he bought the same day as the car, and hiding behind those sunglasses he always wore when he drove—but this time he was driving his rickety old bike. He looked a little odd puffing and pedaling into the school parking lot.

Irving watched Eddie flick down the kickstand to lean his bike into the same space he used to park his car. He smiled and ran up to Eddie.

"Hey, Eddie!" he shouted. "What's up? Where's the car?"

"Didn't do my homework, man," Eddie told Irving.

"Didn't do your homework? Your parents took your car away because you didn't do your homework? Man, that's severe!"

"No way, Irving. That's not what I meant. I didn't do my homework before I bought the car. I ran out of cash. That car took everything. I hadn't figured on a lot of the stuff you've got to pay for if you own a sports car."

When people think about buying a used sports car, it's a good idea for them to think of a line of people standing behind it. These people represent all the other items that have to be bought along with the car. One person carries a briefcase. This person is the insurance agent. Another carries a wrench. That's the mechanic. One stands with forms to be filled out. That's the government. Facing all those people is the buyer, the one handing money to everyone else. As Eddie discovered, if a buyer can't pay these people, that dream sports car will be rumbling down the street with somebody else behind the wheel. The best way to avoid that fate is to do your homework before you pay your money.

The First Step: How Much Can the Buyer Afford?

Before starting the shopping stage, a buyer should ask, "How much money can I afford?" Let's say the buyer can spend $2,000 on a used car. That's the amount of money he or she has in the bank, plus what the person thinks he or she can raise between now and the time of purchase. That $2,000 cannot be spent only on the car, however. The buyer must not forget the incidentals, those little items all drivers need before they get behind the wheel.

The first thing the buyer must figure is the cost of insurance. For teenage drivers, this is an especially big expense. If you don't believe that, call your family insurance agent. Ask how much auto coverage will cost when you become a driver. The agent will want to know what kind of car will be insured, so you should think of a sports car that you especially like. When you name that car to the agent, you might be surprised at how much the coverage would be. Not only would you be paying for being a young, inexperienced driver, but you'd also be paying more for driving a sports car. That's because sports cars are involved in more crashes than other cars. And, because sports cars are lighter than bigger cars, the people in those cars are injured more seriously and the car suffers more damage in a crash. In other words, injuries and damages cost more to repair. That's why insurance companies charge more to cover sports cars.

Let's say an agent has told a car buyer that he or she will pay about $1,000 per year for insurance. Ouch! But then the agent tells the buyer that the payment can be split into two installments of $500 each. Now the buyer knows he or she will need $500 immediately after buying the car and $500 more six months later.

Next, the buyer must figure how much he or she will pay for normal maintenance. The U.S. government says that running the average car takes about 22¢ per mile. (A used sports car might take a little more, but using the 22¢ figure will put the buyer close to the mark.) So, for every ten miles the buyer drives, he or she will be paying about $2.20. If a person drives 50 miles per week—about seven miles per day—it will cost about $11 per week to run the car. That's $44 per month or $528 per year.

Now the writer is telling me the order of items I have to figure in that $2,000. The word *First* is a signal word. I should figure in the cost of insurance first, I guess, because it's a pretty big expense.

Cultural Awareness: Students originally from other countries may wish to tell the class about the most popular cars in their homelands.

Response Clue: Here students may have circled sentences and drawn arrows and underlined *because* and *why* to identify them as words that signal cause-and-effect relationships.

Clarification: You may wish to ask students to reread this paragraph and even do the math themselves in order to clarify the concept of car maintenance.

The word *Next* is a signal. Next, the article says I have to figure in the cost of upkeep—that includes normal maintenance and registration fees.

Meeting Individual Needs: For students who find sidenotes confusing, have them fold back the page and read the selection without the model sidenotes.

Read the rest of the article. Summarize in the margins the sequence, or order, of steps for making a car purchase. Underline signal words where they appear in the article.

Response Clue: The word *finally* may lead students to expect that the list of additional expenses is ending.

Additional Skills: This selection is also appropriate for teaching Drawing Conclusions.

Response Clue: Students may have circled this sentence as an example of cause and effect.

Summarizing: Have students stop reading at this heading and summarize the main ideas of the previous section. Students should include information about the expenses that should be considered in addition to the price of the car.

Finally, the buyer should call the state's department of motor vehicles to find out what fees have to be paid to register the car. The buyer should remember that registration has to be renewed every year. Most states base these fees on the value of the car, but spending between $100 and $200 on registration is fairly typical.

What part of the $2,000 the buyer has set aside can he or she actually count on spending on the car, then? The person should immediately reduce that $2,000 by $500 for the insurance, and by at least one month's worth of operating expenses and registration fees—for a total of about $650. The car the buyer can now afford will cost about $1,400. And if the buyer wants to keep the car for more than a couple of months, he or she had better have quite a bit of extra money budgeted every month for possible repairs!

So, for an idea of what kind of sports car that $1,400 can buy, the buyer can check newspaper advertisements and used car dealers. Obviously, a 1956 gullwing Mercedes Benz—a type of car that sells for about $1 million at auctions—will not be an option, but there may be some used sports cars that are both interesting and affordable for the buyer. The buyer should remember that he or she is *just shopping* at this point. Eddie bought his car at this stage and, well, he's on his Schwinn.

How Can the Buyer Find Out More About Cars?

At the end of the shopping stage, the buyer should narrow the list of affordable, attractive cars to two models. Then he or she should go—guess where? To the library! The buyer is about to engage in some very important research.

Several magazines specialize in writing about cars. The most impartial magazine is *Consumer Reports*. The librarian can help a buyer find this publication's annual *Car Buyer's Guide* for the model year being researched. The guide features every model made during that year. The buyer should compare the cars he or she is researching with other cars. Value, safety, and reliability are important areas to check.

Next, the buyer should look for the *Kelly Blue Book*. This is a directory of every car made. It tells approximately how much each model is worth as it ages and accumulates miles. The suggested price may be a little higher or lower than the car the buyer sees because of variables like how well the previous owner treated the car.

Now the buyer is armed with some valuable information. He or she knows how much the cars are worth according to an independent rating guide, how well the cars were made, and how much the insurance cost will be.

What Should the Buyer Do at the Point of Purchase?

There are several things for a buyer to remember when talking to any automobile salesperson, whether that person works for a dealer or is selling a private car. First, a salesperson's job is to sell a car. A salesperson will always avoid telling the buyer anything that may change his or her mind about wanting the car. Second, the salesperson *has* to sell a car. That's how salespeople earn their living. The buyer should also remember that there are many used cars available. In other words, the salesperson has competition! This means the buyer should stick to the price he or she can pay even if it is a little lower than the salesperson says the car is worth.

The most important thing buyers need to do when talking with a salesperson is to ask many questions. For example: "How many miles does the car have? How many owners has the car had? What work was done to the car to prepare it for sale? Will you warranty the car, or are you selling it 'as is?'" (If the salesperson answers "as is," that means he or she is not responsible for any repairs on the car after the buyer drives it away.) The buyer should also find out if the car has been salvaged. That means the car was involved in a serious accident and was rebuilt. It is never a good idea to buy a car that has been salvaged. Once a car has been "totaled," it is impossible to make it safe again. The buyer can ask the salesperson for written assurance that the car was not salvaged.

How To Buy a Used Sports Car ■ **107**

If a car looks good to the buyer, he or she should ask to drive it. The salesperson will come along. On this test drive, the buyer should be sure to drive the car at a variety of lawful speeds. The buyer might ask to take the car on the highway and also drive it on a neighborhood street. Sports cars should shift smoothly. The clutch should not "stick," or have to be let out almost all the way before allowing the gears to engage. A sports car should also accelerate easily and quickly and should brake without pulling to one side or the other.

Can the Buyer Have a Mechanic Look at the Car?

If the car feels good to the buyer, the next step is to call a trusted mechanic and make an appointment to have the car inspected. This will cost a little money, maybe about $25, but it could save the buyer lots of money later. If the salesperson doesn't want to allow the buyer to take the car to a mechanic, the buyer should firmly state that he or she won't buy the car without an inspection.

A mechanic will check to make sure everything is in working order. The buyer should also ask the mechanic to check for things that might go wrong in the future. For example, are the brake linings worn? Is the radiator corroding? The clutch is especially important to check;

Summarizing: Have students stop at this heading and summarize what a person should look for when test driving a used car.

Additional Skills: This section of the article can also be used to teach the skill of identifying main idea and details (see ATE page 57).

this often wears out in sports cars. If repairs are needed, the buyer should ask for an estimate of how much money these things will cost to fix. That will tell the buyer a truer cost of the car. If, say, a mechanic says $100 worth of repairs will be needed within six months, the buyer knows to add $100 to the real cost of the car.

Finally, the buyer should talk price with the salesperson. Certainly, a price will have been advertised, but is that price close to the *Blue Book* value researched by the buyer? If it is far above the *Blue Book* price, and the salesperson refuses to lower the price, it's time for the buyer to move on. The buyer must never forget that there are hundreds of cars for sale, many of them sports cars. No one should be able to convince a buyer that the car he or she admires is the last one left.

On the other hand, if the price is right, the car is in good condition, and the salesperson has answered all questions satisfactorily, there may be a match! One final word of warning, though, to keep our buyer from ending up like Eddie. Maybe he or she should skip the leather jacket and put that money aside for gas and the next insurance payment.

Meeting Individual Needs:
Ask students having difficulty with cause and effect to describe what a car buyer should do if the salesperson is asking too much for the car. When they answer, point out that they have identified an effect that was caused by the salesperson's refusal to lower the price.

Student Self-Assessment:
Ask students to rate themselves in the following areas on a scale of 1-4, with 1 being the least degree and 4 being the greatest degree: ability to utilize the strategy, ease in writing sidenotes, and ability to transfer skill to reading. (Make clear that student responses are for their own purposes only.)

If you are working on

Lesson 11	Lesson 12
page 98	page 101

Preteaching Vocabulary:
You may wish to preteach the following vocabulary: *lentils, frijoles refritos, tostadas, tortillas.*

Accessing Prior Knowledge: Ask students to discuss what foods might be served at a Mexican restaurant. You may point out that many of the names for these foods are part of our vocabulary today.

Circle sequence signal words wherever they appear. Then, for each recipe, make notes in the margin summarizing the steps for completing each bean dish. Number each step.

Response Clue: Students may have circled several statements in this paragraph to indicate cause-and-effect relationships, and underlined the signal words *as a result* and *because.*

Making Predictions: Ask students to predict what kind of information might be presented in this section.

Response Clue: Students may have noticed that dates are signal words that can help them put events in the proper sequence.

How to Make Tasty, Nutritious Recipes With Beans

by Julie Catalano

Beans have long been a tasty staple of the Latino diet. They are a basic ingredient in many Mexican, South American, Cuban, and Puerto Rican dishes. Today, many people are changing their eating habits. As a result, beans are more popular than ever. Although they were once known as "poor man's meat," there is nothing poor about the nutritional content or taste of beans. In fact, beans are often a healthful replacement for meat in main dishes like soups, stews, casseroles, and chilis. They are an excellent source of protein, are high in fiber, and are packed with vitamins and minerals. In addition, because beans come from plants, they are almost free of fat and have no cholesterol. And all this can be bought for mere pennies a pound!

A Brief History

Where did beans come from? The bean family is a large one, with members scattered all over the world. Its family name is *legume*, which is any of a large group of plants having seeds growing in pods, including beans, peas, and lentils. There are more than 14,000 specimens in the legume family, but only about two dozen are grown for human consumption. If you think all beans are alike, think again. They range from the commonly used navy, kidney, pinto, string, and black beans to the more exotic adzuki, garbanzos, and flageolets. Other varieties are black-eyed peas, red beans, pink beans, and soybeans.

Lentils are probably the oldest cultivated legume, dating from 8000 B.C. Close relatives of lentils are dried split peas, which make delicious soups. You might remember the "pease porridge hot" in the nursery rhyme. That was split pea soup. One of the oldest known beans is the broad, or fava, bean. It dates back to the Bronze Age, around 3000 B.C. These little beans were so highly

BASIC BEANS

Ingredients

    1 cup of dried beans, such as pinto or black
       beans
    3–4 cups water
    One clove of garlic, minced
    A pinch of cumin
    Salt and pepper to taste

Process

    Soaking: First, wash the beans carefully and place them in a large bowl with plenty of water (3 to 4 cups). Leave them to soak overnight. The next day, you will find that the beans have absorbed most of the water and, as a result, have swollen in size. Discard any beans that float to the top. Discard the soaking water and rinse the beans in cool water.

    Cooking: First, place the soaked beans in a large pot and cover with 3 to 4 cups of water. Then add garlic, cumin, salt, and pepper, and bring to a boil. Reduce heat, cover, and simmer until tender, usually one to four hours (two is average). Serve hot. To store, allow beans to cool to room temperature, then refrigerate or freeze. Makes three cups.

    Faster cooking method: Bring beans and water to a boil for two minutes, set aside for one hour. Drain and rinse, and then cook as above.

Response Clue: Students may have noticed that ingredients are listed in the sequence in which they are used. Therefore the list of ingredients can help them figure out the steps in a recipe.

Response Clue: Students might use the signal words *first* and *the next day* from this paragraph to help them determine the sequence of steps for soaking the beans.

Response Clue: Students may have circled part of the second sentence in the paragraph because it contains a cause and effect relationship.

regarded that the ancient Egyptians, Greeks, and Romans used them as offerings for their dead and as an important part of their religious rituals. The Greeks would hold a "bean feast" to honor the mythological god Apollo.

    In the Americas, long before Columbus arrived, Native Americans depended on beans because they are a high-energy food. Some of the groups have long had traditions centered around the bean. The Hopi, for example, hold a bean festival ceremonial every year. The Senecas believe that beans are a gift from the Creator to humankind. Some of the most commonly known beans—kidney, pinto, lima, wax, and snap beans—are native to the Americas and were unknown to Europeans until after Columbus's voyages to South America. In fact, the greatest variety of dried beans came from the Americas and were not a part of the European diet until the 16th century.

Additional Skills: This selection is also appropriate for teaching classification (see ATE page 81).

NATIVE AMERICAN BEAN AND SQUASH CHOWDER

Ingredients

2 cups navy beans, black beans, or pinto beans (see "Basic Beans")
OR
2 cups canned navy beans, black beans, or pinto beans
1 large onion, chopped
2 tablespoons paprika
3 tablespoons olive oil
4 medium fresh or canned tomatoes
1 tablespoon tamari (soy sauce)
1/2 teaspoon oregano
1 acorn squash, peeled, seeded, and chopped
1/2 cup corn kernels

Process

Heat beans in large pot. Meanwhile, saute onion and paprika together in olive oil for about 5-7 minutes. Then add tomatoes, tamari, and oregano and cook until well blended. Next, add this mixture and chopped squash to the beans and cook until squash begins to disintegrate. Finally, add corn and cook for 5 minutes. Serve in soup plates. Makes 4-6 servings.

TOSTADAS DE FRIJOLES (BEAN TOSTADAS)

Ingredients

1 cup canned refried beans, or follow recipe for "Frijoles Refritos" on page 115
1 teaspoon vegetable oil
6 pre-packaged tostada shells
1/2 cup shredded low-fat cheddar cheese
1 cup shredded lettuce
1 large tomato, chopped
Picante sauce or salsa (optional)

Process

First, heat the beans thoroughly in a saucepan for about 5 minutes. Add vegetable oil if needed to thin the beans. Divide beans into six servings. Spread one serving on each tostada shell. Then add shredded cheese, lettuce, and tomato. Top with picante sauce. Makes six servings.

The early settlers in this country learned much from the Native Americans about how to grow and use beans. One of their most common dishes—succotash, a mixture of beans and corn—remains popular to this day. The settlers of colonial Massachusetts learned how to bake beans from the Indians, and Boston baked beans are world famous.

Summarizing: Have students stop reading here and summarize historical facts about beans presented in the preceding section.

Nutritional Advantages

If there was ever a food that tasted good and was good for you, it's the bean. All beans have virtually the same number of calories—about 100 per half cup cooked—and about five grams of total fiber. Beans are considered substantial sources of calcium, iron, potassium, phosphorous, zinc, magnesium, and B vitamins.

Medical research continues to confirm the health benefits of beans, most notably in the prevention of heart disease. Cooked beans are a rich source of soluble fiber. In one study, dry beans were found to be as effective in lowering cholesterol as oat bran. Another study found that one cup of canned beans in tomato sauce each day lowers cholesterol about 10 percent after 21 days.

One thing that is surprising about beans as compared to other vegetables is the fact that canned varieties are almost as healthful and nutritious as freshly prepared beans. Still, nothing beats the taste of homemade beans—whether they are eaten as a main dish, a side vegetable, or as an ingredient in other ethnic recipes.

Additional Skills: This selection is also appropriate for teaching Fact and Opinion (see ATE page 60).

TEX-MEX BEAN AND CHEESE TACOS

Ingredients

  2 cups refried beans (see "Frijoles Refritos")
    OR
  1 16-oz can refried beans
  8 packaged flour tortillas or corn tortillas
  1 cup shredded low-fat cheddar cheese

Process

Heat tortillas on a griddle, turning until thoroughly heated. Transfer to a plate and cover with a towel to keep warm. Then heat refried beans on a stove or in a microwave. Spoon 2 tablespoons beans into tortilla, top with shredded cheese, and fold tortilla in half. Makes eight.

Cultural Awareness: Discuss the phrase "Tex-Mex" and how it connotes the blending of Mexican and Texan cultures. Ask students to suggest other examples of blended cultures, such as the Chinatowns in some United States cities.

ESL/LEP: Students may
want to write the steps in this
recipe in their first language
before writing it in English.

Cultural Awareness:
Students may want to share
favorite recipes from their
own cultures with the class.

Response Clue: You may
want to review students'
margin notes next to the
recipes to see if they have
listed and numbered the
steps correctly.

Meeting Individual Needs:
Use this Process section to
help students identify the
three steps in making
Mexican rice and beans.

MEXICAN RICE AND BEANS

Ingredients

2 cups brown rice
1 onion, chopped
1 tomato, chopped
1/2 green pepper, chopped
1 garlic clove, diced
Pinch of salt
1 teaspoon basil
3 cups water
1 cup cooked pinto, kidney, or black beans
   OR
One 10- or 12-ounce can pinto, kidney, or
   black beans
2 tablespoons salsa or picante sauce

Process

Cook rice, onion, pepper, garlic, salt, and basil in
3 cups water over low to medium heat. When all
liquid is absorbed (about 45 minutes), stir in the
beans and salsa or picante sauce and simmer an
additional 10 minutes. Add more salsa to taste, if
desired. Serves 3-4.

Cultural Awareness: Have
students describe similar
foods from their own
cultures.

Cultural Awareness: Ask
students whose first language
is Spanish to help others
learn the pronunciation of
Mexican words in the article.

Cooking with Beans

Of the many kinds of beans used in Latino recipes,
three are particularly easy to find. One is the large red
bean called a kidney because of its shape. The second is
the black bean, or turtle bean, native to South America
and boiled, fried, spiced, and mixed with rice and other
foods. Black beans have a nutty, earthy flavor and are
traditionally made into black bean soup in Cuba, Puerto
Rico, and Spain.

The third, and most commonly used bean in Latino
cooking is the *pinto*, the Spanish word for "painted."
These beans have spots of brownish-pink on their skin,
just like the horse with the same name. When cooked, the
pinto has a soft, smooth texture turning dark pink in
color, and a hearty, full-bodied flavor. This is the bean
used to make *frijoles refritos*, or refried beans, and is also
used in traditional rice and bean recipes.

Cooking beans is not a difficult or complicated task.
The most important thing to remember about dried
beans, such as pintos, is that they must be soaked before
cooking in order to replace water lost in the drying

FRIJOLES REFRITOS (REFRIED BEANS)

Ingredients

1 cup (8 oz.) pinto beans (see "Basic Beans")
OR
1 cup canned kidney beans
1/2 onion, finely chopped
2 tablespoons of vegetable oil
1 whole green chile, finely chopped

Process

First, place the beans in a food processor and make them into a thick paste. Or, mash them by hand with a potato masher, adding a small amount of vegetable oil if needed. Next, lightly fry the onion and the chile in the oil. When they are soft, add the mashed beans. Finally, stir until they are thoroughly mixed and hot. Makes two half-cup servings. Refrigerate leftovers and reheat the next day in the microwave or on the stove.

Quick Mexican Bean Dip: Add chopped jalapeño peppers, tabasco sauce, or chili pepper sauce to refried beans. Heat and mix thoroughly. Serve with corn chips or tortilla chips.

process. Then they must be thoroughly cooked so that they are tender. Proper soaking and cooking also aids in the digestibility of beans. Cooking times can vary from one to four hours, with two being about average. Lentils and split peas are unique to the legume family in that they require no soaking and have shorter cooking times.

The traditional method involves adding six cups of water to every pound of dry beans and soaking the beans overnight or for eight hours before draining and cooking. For a faster soaking time, bring beans and water to a boil for two minutes, set the pot aside for one hour, and then drain and cook. The fastest cooking method of all is to open a can of beans! To choose the canned beans that will be best for your health, however, remember to avoid those packed in fat and those with too much salt. Beans are best prepared naturally with generous helpings of herbs and spices which add lots of flavor but no calories or fat.

Here is some bean math to help you figure serving sizes: One cup of dry beans is equal to about three cups cooked. One pound of dry beans is equal to six cups

Response Clue: Students may want to make lists of the sequence of steps in each category of *traditional, faster,* and *fastest* methods, and then compare them.

Response Clue: Students may need to use their own prior knowledge and experiences to understand the effects that eating canned beans high in fat and salt might have.

cooked. One 12-1/2-ounce can equals about one-and-one-third cups of beans.

Fresh dried beans are best cooked in large batches. This is especially true of the pinto bean, the bean used in making *frijoles refritos*, or refried beans. The reason for this is that refried beans can be used in many recipes. In Mexico, preparing refried beans is one of the most common ways to cook beans. The process does not really include frying the beans twice as the name suggests, however. Beans are often simply prepared as described on Sunday and then refrigerated and reheated during the week as needed. A little more vegetable oil is added each time.

Try one of these simple recipes for preparing your very own lean bean cuisine. *Buen provecho!* Enjoy!

Student Self-Assessment:
Ask students to rate themselves in the following areas on a scale of 1-4, with 1 being the least degree and 4 being the greatest degree: ability to utilize the strategy, ease in writing sidenotes, and ability to transfer skill to reading. (Make clear that student responses are for their own purposes only.)

If you are working on

Lesson 11	Lesson 12
↓	↓
page **117**	page **119**

Reviewing *Sequence*

A. Read the article "How to Make Tasty, Nutritious Recipes with Beans" on pages 110-116. Underline signal words and note in the margins the steps for completing the recipes. Then use your notes in response to one of the recipes to complete the chart below.

Reviewing the Strategy: To complete the graphic organizer, have students refer to the sidenotes they wrote on pages 110-116 and the words they underlined in the text. Explain that they may use short phrases to describe the steps in the recipes rather than complete sentences.

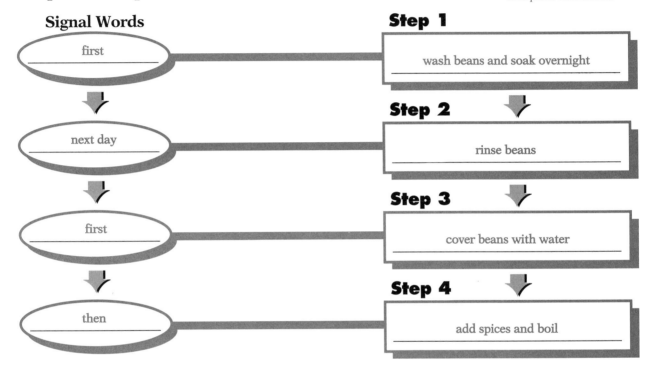

Signal Words

first → **Step 1** wash beans and soak overnight

next day → **Step 2** rinse beans

first → **Step 3** cover beans with water

then → **Step 4** add spices and boil

B. Think of something you know how to make. Then write directions for making it. Use signal words so that your reader will understand the sequence of steps in your directions.

Peer Sharing: After students complete Section B, have them share their recipes with a partner. Have partners evaluate one another's recipes.

Accept all appropriate directions that list steps in proper sequence. Check to make

sure students have included signal words.

Testing **Sequence**

Test-Taking Hints:
Suggest to students
that when a test asks
for a written response,
they may want to first
jot down their ideas on
a piece of scrap paper
before writing the
answer on the test
page.

A. Rewrite each statement so that it reflects the sequence for each recipe.

1. According to the basic bean recipe, first, bring the beans to a boil, then soak them overnight, and finally, add garlic, cumin, salt, and pepper.

According to the basic bean recipe, first, soak the beans overnight. Then add garlic,

cumin, salt and pepper, and finally bring to a boil.

2. To make refried beans, do the following: Fry the dry beans in oil with the chile. Then, place the beans and chili in a food processor until the beans form a thick paste.

To make refried beans, do the following: First, place the beans in a food processor

and make them into a thick paste. Then, fry the beans in oil with the chili.

3. To make Tex-Mex Bean and Cheese Tacos, spoon 2 tablespoons beans into tortilla, top with shredded cheese, and heat on a griddle.

First, heat the tacos on a griddle, then spoon two tablespoons beans onto each taco,

and finally top with shredded cheese.

**Assessing Student
Writing:** Rate student
writing on a scale of 1-
4, with 1 being the least
degree and 4 being the
greatest degree. Use
the following criteria:
originality,
organization,
reasoning, and clarity.

B. Write a recipe of your own for something you make every day. Use signal words to show the correct order of the steps.

Accept all recipe directions that use signal words to show sequence.

**To begin
Lesson 12**

**page
101**

Reviewing *Cause and Effect*

A. Reread the article "How to Make Tasty, Nutritious Recipes with Beans." As you read, circle any causes and effects stated in the article. Underline any signal words. Then, use some of the words you have circled and underlined to fill in the diagram below.

Reviewing the Strategy: Have students complete the diagram according to the directions provided, using the causes and effects they have circled in the text as well as the underlined signal words. Remind students that a cause is a reason for something and an effect is a result.

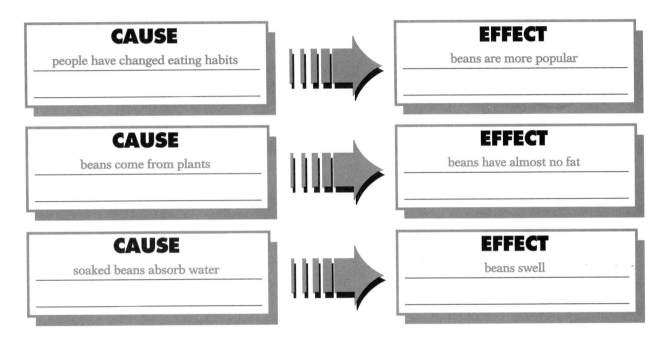

CAUSE
people have changed eating habits

EFFECT
beans are more popular

CAUSE
beans come from plants

EFFECT
beans have almost no fat

CAUSE
soaked beans absorb water

EFFECT
beans swell

B. Think of a cause-and-effect relationship you learned about in a science class, a home economics class, or another class. On the lines below, write a short paragraph describing it in detail. You may wish to make a diagram like the one above to help explain the relationship.

Lesson Management: Answers in the graphic organizer are suggestions. Student may suggest additional answers.

Accept any appropriate responses that show students have properly identified a

cause-and-effect relationship.

Student Self-Assessment: Students might wish to evaluate their own writing on a scale of 1-4, with 1 being the least degree and 4 being the greatest degree. Have them use the following criteria: Did I answer the question? Did I use examples from the text? Are my ideas clearly stated?

Testing Cause and Effect

A. The incomplete statements below are based on the article "How to Make Tasty, Nutritious Recipes with Beans." Circle the letter next to the word that best completes the statement. Then, on the line provided, tell if the answer is a cause or an effect.

1. As a result of the high regard ancient people had for the fava bean, they

    a. called them broad beans.
    (b.) used them in religious rituals.
    c. made succotash.
    d. prepared them with oat bran.

An effect.

2. Proper soaking and cooking results in beans that are

    (a.) digestible.
    b. unique.
    c. refried.
    d. salty.

An effect.

3. According to the author, studies have shown that eating a daily serving of canned beans in tomato sauce will

    a. lead to excessive weight gain.
    (b.) lower cholesterol after 21 days.
    c. be very expensive.
    d. take too long to prepare.

An effect.

4. Most beans need to be soaked before cooking because

    a. they are cooked in large batches.
    b. they are called pinto beans.
    c. they should be cooked with herbs.
    (d.) they lose water when they are dried.

A cause.

B. In your own words, write a paragraph that describes why including beans in your diet is a good idea.

Accept any reasonable responses that explain the beneficial effects of including beans in one's diet.

Unit SEVEN

BECOMING AN ACTIVE READER

Effective readers take an active part when reading **poetry**. This means that they respond to a poem emotionally by asking: How does it make me feel? How has the poet used words to make me feel this way?

Using Skills and Strategies

Reading poems aloud will help you listen for the ways that poets use sound to add meaning to poems. You might ask: What **sound** devices does the poet use? How do those sound devices help bring **meaning** to the poem?

Looking for relationships among words is another way to become actively involved in reading poetry. Sometimes poets use words that can be used to make **analogies.** Analogies are special word relationships in which one pair of words is related to each other and to another pair in the same way.

In this unit, the skills of **sound and meaning** and identifying word relationships to form **analogies** will help you become an effective reader.

Reading Poems

Poetry is a special form of literature. In poetry, every word and sound counts. Thoughts, feelings, moods, and emotions are all expressed through a few words. Poetry is meant to be read aloud so that you can hear the sounds and rhythms that the words make.

Responding to Poems

Good readers look for ways that poets use words. They notice how sound devices create meaning in a poem. They think about these devices as they respond to poetry. Jot down your feelings and thoughts as you read the two poems in this unit: "The Alarm Clock" and "My Father's Song." Writing responses will help you become involved in the poems. Discuss your responses to the poems with your classmates.

Unit Enrichment: Invite students to "publish" the poems they write in this unit. Students can copy their poems in final form, checking spelling and punctuation. They can then bind all the poems together to make a classroom poetry book. Invite several students to design a book cover with a title for their classroom anthology. You might wish to duplicate the book and send it home to parents.

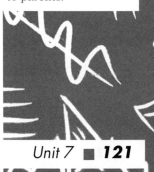

Sound and Meaning

| Lesson 13 | Introducing page 122 | Practicing page 123 | Applying page 124 | Reviewing page 132 | Testing page 133 |

Lesson Objective: To relate sound and meaning in the poems "The Alarm Clock" and "My Father's Song" by using a cluster diagram.

Oral Language: Allow time for students to read aloud some favorite poems from a collection of their choice. Students should share with classmates what they like about the poems they've chosen.

ESL/LEP: Invite students to recite simple poems or rhymes from their first languages. Students might enjoy clapping or tapping their fingers during the recitation in order to emphasize the rhythm of poetry. Point out devices such as repetition and pattern of stressed and unstressed syllables.

Modeling the Strategy: Model responding to sound and meaning as you read lines from one of your favorite poems. Refer to the cluster diagram. After completing this page, have students copy the diagram on page 132 in their notebooks and apply it to the poems in this unit.

Managing the Lesson: Students can read aloud the poems with a partner or in a small group. Remind students to use the sidenotes to answer questions 1 and 2. The sidenotes show how active readers use sound devices to determine meaning in poems.

Introducing Strategies

One way to enjoy poetry is to listen for ways **sounds** of the words add **meaning**. Some sound devices poets use include:

- **rhythm,** a pattern of stressed and unstressed syllables;
- **repetition,** repeating words or phrases;
- **alliteration,** using words with the same first consonant sound;
- **sound words,** words that sound like what they mean;
- **"soft"** or **"loud" words,** such as *velvet* or *siren;*
- **short words** that make choppy sounds.

The cluster below shows how you might think about **sound** and **meaning** while reading poetry.

Reading the Poem

Read aloud the poems "The Alarm Clock" and "My Father's Song" and the sidenotes on pages 128-129. Then complete the items below.

1. List two sound devices that the reader identified.

In "The Alarm Clock," the reader identified a "loud" word and short lines. In "My

Father's Song," the reader identified rhythm and alliteration.

2. Explain how each of these devices helped add meaning.

Students may suggest that the reader felt startled by the loudness and felt jumpy

from the one-word lines.

Practicing **Sound and Meaning**

A. The following statements are about the poems "The Alarm Clock" and "My Father's Song" on pages 128-129. Circle the letter of the choice that best completes each statement. Then on the lines provided, tell why you made each choice.

1. In "The Alarm Clock," the poet gives meaning to the harsh sound of the alarm clock by relating it to

    a. waking up   c. the drugstore
        in the morning.   incident.
    b. daydreaming.   d. none of the above.

The incident in the drugstore is harsh and startling. The poet says that the sound of

the alarm clock reminds her of that incident.

2. It's likely that the poet repeated the *s* sound in "My Father's Song" to suggest

    a. softness.   c. quietness.
    b. sadness.   d. all of the above.

The *s* sound emphasizes all these qualities in the poem.

3. In "My Father's Song," phrases such as *his voice, his song,* and *my father saying things* might tell the reader that the poet misses

    a. the soft mice.   c. the sound of his father's voice.
    b. the feeling of the   d. planting corn.
        soft sand.

The phrases all refer to the voice of the speaker's father.

B. Write a short paragraph in which you explain what happened in the drugstore. In your paragraph, tell how the poet used sound in "The Alarm Clock" to help show her feelings about what happened.

Accept all appropriate responses in which students relate sound devices to the

feelings that the poet expresses in the poem.

Purpose: The purpose of the **Practicing** page is to help students identify sound and meaning in poetry.

Cultural Awareness: Invite students to compare the backgrounds of poets Mari Evans and Simon J. Ortiz. How are their backgrounds different? How are they the same?

Cooperative Learning: Have students work in groups of three to complete the page. One student can read the examples while another acts as the moderator, encouraging each group member to share responses. The third student can be the recorder.

ESL/LEP: You may wish to read the poems aloud to students one more time before they complete the page. Listening to the correct pronunciation of words in the poems will help them identify sound devices.

Writing Process: Before students begin writing, they may wish to go back to the **Introducing** page and review the sound devices poets often use.

Applying *Sound and Meaning*

A. Read the following lines twice, once silently and once out loud. As you read, notice how the writer has used sound to create meaning. Then answer the questions that follow.

Battering the shore,
breakers boom and thunder
then shatter
into whispering foam
melting at my feet.

Battering the shore,
breakers burst and crash
washing away
silent footprints
as shining waves retreat.

1. List sound devices the poet has used in the poem.

Students might list the sound devices of rhythm, repetition, alliteration, sound words,

"soft" or "loud" words, and short lines.

2. For each device, explain how it adds meaning to the poem.

Accept any appropriate responses that demonstrate how sound devices help add

meaning to the poem.

B. Think of a place you would like to describe. Write a short poem using sound as a way to add meaning to the poem.

Accept all appropriate responses. Poems do not have to rhyme or have a regular

beat. However, students should use at least one sound device to add meaning to

their poems.

To review

⬇

page
132

Analogies

Introducing Strategies

Poets think carefully about the words they use and the relationships between words. Good readers look for word relationships to help them understand the poet's ideas. An **analogy** is a special way to look at relationships between words. The analogy below contains words from the poem "My Father's Song." The analogy is written first as a sentence and then in a style you may have seen on tests.

> **Brush IS TO painting AS plow IS TO furrow.**
>
> ___brush___ : ___painting___ :: ___plow___ : ___furrow___

In an analogy, the first two words are related in the same way as the second two words. If a brush is used to make a painting, then a plow must be used to make a furrow. Other relationships include:

- **part and whole** *(map : atlas :: recipe : cookbook);*
- **characteristics** *(fragrant : flower :: towering : tree);*
- **opposites** *(clumsy : graceful :: plain : decorated);*
- **similar meanings** *(moist : damp :: parched : dry);*
- **action to object** *(smolder : fire :: drizzle : rain);*
- **living thing and place** *(spider : web :: fox : den).*

Reading the Poems

Reread the poems "The Alarm Clock" and "My Father's Song" and circle and draw arrows between related words. Then complete the analogy below with a word from "My Father's Song." Finally, name the relationship.

1. stumble : foot :: catch : _____voice_____

2. Relationship: _____action to object_____

Lesson Objective: To identify and write analogies using colon notations and words from the poems "The Alarm Clock" and "My Father's Song."

ESL/LEP: Invite students to read the analogy silently. Then have them read the analogy aloud with the colon notations, using the words *is to* whenever they see a single colon and *as* when they see the double colon. Then have available groups of actual items or pictures of familiar items that are related. Invite students to work on their own or with a partner to create analogies using the names of the items. If necessary, students may write or say the analogy in their first languages.

Modeling the Strategy: Model how to write an analogy with colon notations using words from students' every day vocabulary. Try to use one word in each analogy that will "stretch" their thinking.

Practicing Analogies

A. Circle the letter in front of the word that best completes each analogy. Then on the line provided, identify the relationship.

1. _____ : tremble :: gather : scoop

   (a.) quiver   c. movement
   b. composure   d. width

   Relationship: ___similar meanings___

2. mouse : _____ :: wolf : lair

   a. animal   (c.) burrow
   b. home   d. small

   Relationship: ___living thing and place___

3. furrow : field :: _____ : face

   (a.) wrinkle   c. trench
   b. forehead   d. chin

   Relationship: ___characteristics___

4. hidden : concealed :: unearthed : _____

   a. protected   c. covered
   (b.) uncovered   d. buried

   Relationship: ___similar meanings___

5. soil : sand :: pasture : _____

   a. crest   c. valley
   b. cliff   (d.) field

   Relationship: ___similar meanings___

B. Select two words from the poems. Use them to make up analogies. Write each analogy on the lines below. Then write how the word pairs are related.

___clock___ : ___time___ :: ___calendar___ : ___date___

Relationship: ___object and function___

___sand___ : ___beach___ :: ___rocks___ : ___cliff___

Relationship: ___material and location___

Applying *Analogies*

Read the passage below. Use a word from the passage to complete each analogy that follows. Then name the relationship upon which the analogy is based.

First came an angry storm, full of rage. By dawn, it was gone. The sun rose, brilliant, just above the horizon. The once cloudy sky was now clear. When I got there, the field shone like a million twinkling lights, each blade of grass still beaded with moisture. At each step, I sank slightly into the muddy earth. The fragrance of the rich, black soil rose about me, and I breathed it in. I closed my eyes, glad I was here at last!

1. _____cloudy;_____ : clear :: angry : calm

   Relationship: _____opposites_____

2. _____muddy;_____ : earth :: sandy : beach

   Relationship: _____characteristics_____

3. bead : _____moisture;_____ :: drop : dew

   Relationship: _____characteristics_____

4. _____breathed;_____ : fragrance :: heard : thunder

   Relationship: _____object/action_____

5. dusk : _____dawn;_____ :: brilliant : dull

   Relationship: _____opposites_____

6. partially : slightly :: _____glad;_____ :: delighted

   Relationship: _____similar meanings_____

7. fell : rain :: _____rose;_____ : sun

   Relationship: _____object/action_____

Applying the Skill to Other Disciplines: Have students look for word relationships in advertisements, forms they fill out, or songs they listen to. Encourage them to practice writing analogies using words from those sources.

Peer Sharing: Invite students to read the passage independently and then complete the page with a partner. Both students should be able to name the relationship between the words in each analogy.

ESL/LEP: You may wish to read the passage aloud for students before they complete the analogies. You might also have students restate the passage in English in their own words. Make sure students understand the meaning of the passage before completing the analogies.

To review

↓

page
134

Preteaching Vocabulary:
You may wish to preteach the following vocabulary words: *mornin'*, *remind*, *hangin'*.

Making Predictions: Invite students to predict what the poem is about after they read the title and the headnote.

Mari Evans is a teacher and a poet. Much of Evans's work reflects her concern for the lives of African Americans in a country that has not always treated all citizens equally. The poem below addresses an unlawful practice that existed in the United States as recently as the 1960s. This practice was to exclude African Americans from public places.

The Alarm Clock

by Mari Evans

The notes in the margin show what one reader noticed about sound and meaning. Write your own thoughts about sound and meaning as you read.

Loud is a sound word and it's on a line by itself. That makes me say it more loudly. It's as if the loudness has startled the speaker.

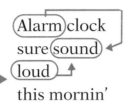

Alarm clock
sure sound
loud
this mornin'

remind me of the time
I sat down
in a drug store
with my mind
a way far off

Response Clue: Circling reflects related words students may have identified in the poem.

until the girl
and she was small
it seems to me
with yellow hair
a hangin'
smiled up and said
'I'm sorry but
we don't serve

Response Clue: Students may note the repetition of the s sound which builds tension here.

you people
here'
and I woke up
quick
like I did this mornin'
when the
alarm
went off

These short lines and one-word lines make the poem sound harsh, jumpy, annoying—like the ringing of the alarm.

It don't do
to wake up
quick

Additional Skills: This poem is also appropriate for teaching Drawing Conclusions. Have students discuss what the poet is saying in the last stanza.

Simon Ortiz (1941-) was raised in the Acoma Pueblo community of New Mexico. He attended several schools and colleges, but feels that his real education came from learning the ways of his Native American culture. Ortiz's work helps gives readers an understanding of that heritage. In this poem, the speaker recalls a family story.

My Father's Song

by Simon J. Ortiz

Wanting to say things,
I miss my father tonight.
His voice, the slight catch,
the depth from his thin chest,
the tremble of emotion
in something he has just said
to his son, his song:

We planted corn one spring at Acu—
we planted several times
but this one particular time
I remember the soft damp sand
in my hand.

My father had stopped at one point
to show me an overturned furrow;
the plowshare had unearthed
the burrow nest of a mouse
in the soft moist sand.

Very gently, he scooped tiny pink animals
into the palm of his hand
and told me to touch them.
We took them to the edge
of the field and put them in the shade
of a sand moist clod.

I remember the very softness
of cool and warm sand and tiny alive mice
and my father saying things.

Preteaching Vocabulary:
You may wish to preteach the following vocabulary words: *catch, tremble, furrow, plowshare, burrow, clod.*

Motivating Question: As students read "My Father's Song," ask them why they think the poet described the incident with the mice when remembering his father.

These notes show one reader's thoughts about sound and meaning in "My Father's Song." As you read, make some notes of your own.

◄ The first stanza has a regular rhythm of stressed and unstressed syllables. It's almost like a ceremonial chant in honor of the speaker's father, especially line 2.

Response Clue: Circles and arrows reflect word relationships students may have identified.

◄ There are a lot of *s* words here. The letter *s* makes a soft sound like the sand and the song. Perhaps the poet is feeling sad.

Response Clue: Students might say that the *s* words add a "soft" sound to the poem.

Response Clue: Students might note the part/whole word relationship: *furrow is to field as palm is to hand.*remembering his father.

Cultural Awareness: Students might enjoy sharing poems and stories from their own culture and heritage.

If you are working on

Lesson 13	Lesson 14
↓	↓
page 122	**page 125**

Preteaching Vocabulary:
Preteach the following words:
exile, immigrant, shiners,
satchel, shanks, wield,
sentinels, excursions, vigor.

Motivating Question:
Ask students why it is
important to remember
important people in our
lives—family or friends—as
we grow older.

As you read the poem,
make notes about
sound and meaning.
Use the wide margin for
your notes.

Response Clue: Students
might note that the
repetition of *Remember* and *I*
remember adds a tone of
reverence to the poem.

Cultural Awareness: Invite
students to name members
of their families who came to
America as immigrants.

Response Clue: These short
lines emphasize the vitality
of the man in the poem.

Response Clue: Students
might note that the repeated
s sound in the words
swimming, sunset, satchel,
stepladders, stretch, and *doze*.
add a soft, nostalgic tone.

Response Clue: Underlining
and arrows reflect word
relationships students may
have identified.

ESL/LEP: If you notice that
students are having difficulty
reading the poem, you may
wish to tape the entire poem
and have them follow along
as they listen to the
recording.

Diana H. Melhem is a writer, poet, and teacher who lives in
New York City. Much of her poetry is about her family life and
the neighborhood in which she lives. This poem is dedicated to
Melhem's own daughter and son.

Grandfather: Frailty Is Not the Story

by Diana H. Melhem

Remember your grandfather tall and straight
Remember him swimming in deep water
Remember his stories of exile and travel
    and immigrant dreams
Remember his ship models designed from memory
Remember him netting shiners with you in Gardiner's
        Bay
    or digging for clams
    or cleaning a fish
    or driving us fast
    to catch the sunset at Maidstone.

I remember him climbing the stairs
    after all the stairs he had climbed
    with his satchel of fabrics
I remember him on stepladders in the Depression
    or holding my hand on the way to school
    me proud of him in his overalls
I remember watching for him at six o'clock
    he would lift me at the door
and then we would sit over roast lamb shanks or
        chicken
and my mother would relate the family news.
Afterwards he would rise to "stretch his legs,"
    read the paper, and doze.

And I remember discussions, the arguments over
          politics
     how he taught me to reason, to wield logic
     as he had done when captain of the debating
               team
     in Tripoli Boys' School, Lebanon
     and the photos of him there, where he was
               becoming
     the tallest and handsomest man in the town.

I remember the pipes arrayed like sentinels on a
               cabinet
the talk of building or buying a boat
explanations of algebra, which I learned to enjoy
and the excursions—
     walking over Brooklyn Bridge into Chinatown
     walking down Ocean Parkway to Sheepshead Bay
or later in a Ford, the three of us, singing
     of the San Fernando Valley
     where we would settle down
     and never more roam.

Remember your grandfather
in his vigor
and that a loving life
takes imagination.

Response Clue: Students might mention the repetition of the word *walking,* which indicates the passage of time. They might say that *singing of the San Fernando Valley* adds a light, lyrical touch to the poem.

Response Clue: The word *bridge* is related to *water* in the same way as the word *parkway* is related to *land.*

If you are working on

Lesson 13 | Lesson 14

page 132 | page 134

Reviewing *Sound and Meaning*

Reviewing the Strategy: Have students refer to their sidenotes and circled words on pages 130-131 to complete the cluster diagram.

A. Read the poem "Grandfather: Frailty Is Not the Story" twice, once silently and once out loud. As you read, circle words that show sound devices and note how they add meaning to the poem. Use the circled words and your notes to complete the diagram below.

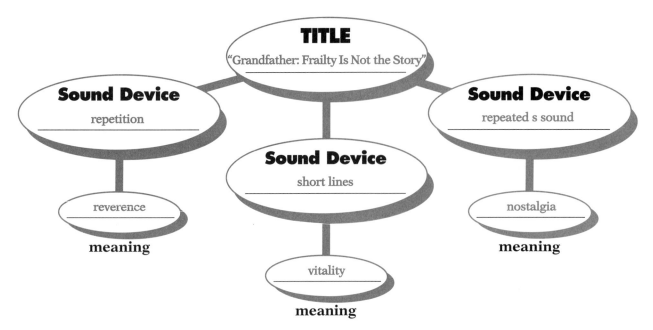

TITLE
"Grandfather: Frailty Is Not the Story"

Sound Device
repetition

reverence
meaning

Sound Device
short lines

vitality
meaning

Sound Device
repeated s sound

nostalgia
meaning

Peer Sharing: Invite partners to compare the explanations they wrote. How does their partner's explanation help them better understand the poem?

Student Self-Assessment: Students might wish to evaluate their own writing on a scale of 1-4, with 1 being the least degree and 4 being the greatest degree. Have them use the following criteria: Did I answer the question? Did I use examples from the text? Are my ideas clearly stated?

B. In your own words, explain how the sounds and words in the poem create a certain image of the man described in the poem.

Accept all appropriate responses in which students relate sounds and words in the

poem to the grandfather's image. For example, students may describe the grandfather

as being a man of action because of such words as *swimming, digging, cleaning,*

_____

_____

_____

_____

_____

_____

_____

Testing Sound and Meaning

Test-Taking Hints:
Students should keep in mind that although they are to fill in only the circles next to the statements that make sense, they need to write an explanation for each of the examples.

Meeting Individual Needs:
Students who find it challenging to master the skill of identifying sound and meaning may need to go back and read the poem several times before completing this page.

A. Each statement below is about sound and meaning in the poem "Grandfather: Frailty Is Not the Story." Fill in the circle next to each statement that makes sense. Then, on the lines provided, explain why you did or did not fill in each bubble.

1. Repetition of words such as *Remember* and *I remember* help show the poet's respect for her father.

The poet's respect for her father is evident when she tells her children to remember

him and when she herself remembers all the good qualities he had.

2. The short lines *or digging for clams/or cleaning a fish/or driving us fast* emphasize Grandfather's vigor.

Students should fill in the circle because these activities are ones that might be done by

a vigorous person who is full of life.

3. The *s* sounds in *singing of the San Fernando Valley where we would settle down* add a nervous, fearful tone to the poem.

Students should not fill in the circle because the *s* sounds bring a light, lyrical tone to

the poem rather than a nervous, fearful tone.

4. In the last stanza of the poem, the *l* sounds in *loving life* add a soft, musical sound to the poem.

Students should fill in the circle because the letter *l* sound in the words can be

interpreted as having a soft, musical sound.

B. Write a brief poem about someone special you would like remembered. Try to use sound to add meaning to your poem.

Accept all responses based on remembrances of a special person. Students should

include at least one example of a sound device in their poem.

ESL/LEP: If students feel more comfortable dictating their poetry to a writing partner or other classmate, encourage them to do so.

To begin
Lesson 14
↓
page
125

Reviewing *Analogies*

A. Reread the poem "Grandfather: Frailty Is Not the Story" on pages 130-131 and circle words that show relationships. Then use each group of words below to write an analogy.

1. sentinel, algebra, satchel, guard, bag

| sentinel | : | guard | :: | satchel | : | bag |

2. vigor, reason, emotion, frailty, immigrant

| vigor | : | frailty | :: | reason | : | emotion |

3. settle, resolve, wander, roam, locate

| settle | : | wander | :: | locate | : | roam |

B. What is the relationship between the word *Frailty* in the title and the rest of the poem? Use examples from the poem in your response.

Accept all appropriate responses that include examples from the poem.

_____

_____

_____

_____

_____

_____

_____

_____

Testing *Analogies*

A. Read the pairs of analogies in each item below. Only one of the analogies in each pair is correct. Fill in the circle in front of the correct analogy. Then name the relationship on which the correct analogy is based.

1. ● immigrant : newcomer :: exiled : banished
   ○ immigrant : native :: exiled : banished
   Relationship: _____ similar meanings _____

2. ○ shiners : water :: clams : mollusks
   ● shiners : water :: clams : sand
   Relationship: _____ living thing and place _____

3. ○ doze : slumber :: proud : ashamed
   ● doze : awaken :: proud : ashamed
   Relationship: _____ opposites _____

4. ○ excursion : ticket :: argument : debater
   ● excursion : trip :: argument : debate
   Relationship: _____ similar meanings _____

5. ● rung : stepladder :: shank : lamb
   ○ rung : stepladder :: animal : lamb
   Relationship: _____ part and whole _____

6. ○ relate : report :: descend : climb
   ● relate : report :: ascend : climb
   Relationship: _____ similar meanings _____

B. Make up an analogy using the word *captain*. Write your analogy as a sentence in the shaded section of the box below. Then write it in testing style.

> Accept any analogy with the word *captain*. Make sure the first two words in students' analogies are related in the same way as the second two words.
>
> _____ : _____ :: _____ : _____

Test-Taking Hints:
Point out that students should completely fill in the circle next to each correct analogy. Remind them to write the name of the relationship upon which the analogy is based.

Meeting Individual Needs:
Students who find analogies challenging might wish to review the list of analogy relationships shown on the **Introducing** page before they complete the test.

ESL/LEP: Have students who are newcomers to the United States and are unfamiliar with English vocabulary make up analogies using words from their first languages.

Unit EIGHT

BECOMING AN ACTIVE READER

Good readers are curious about the lives of the poets whose **poems** they read. They ask questions about the experiences that may have led the poet to write the poems. They look for answers to their questions as they read.

Using Skills and Strategies

Learning about a poet's **cultural background** can add to your understanding and appreciation of a poem. You might ask: What do I know about the poet's culture? How is that culture reflected in the poem? What experiences have I had that are similar or different?

Identifying the **tone** of a poem also can help you to understand the poet's message. You might ask: How does the poet's attitude toward the subject affect my response?

In this unit, recognizing **cultural background** and identifying **tone** will help you read more actively.

The Poem: The Writer's Voice

Poetry from all cultures instructs and entertains us. Reading poems written by people from other cultures can help you define who you are. While the history of each culture is different, people are connected through emotions—we all experience anger and joy, sadness and love. The voices of poetry give us a way to experience that connection.

Responding to Poems

Good readers are sometimes so moved by a poem that it seems they've actually talked with the poet. In a way, they have. As you read "Leaves," "Thirst," "Lineage," and "Incident," be aware of the experiences and feelings that the poems bring to your mind. Jot down notes in the margins of things you'd like to share in person with each poet. Use these notes to discuss the poems with your classmates.

Cultural Context

| Lesson 15 | Introducing page 137 | Practicing page 138 | Applying page 139 | Reviewing page 148 | Testing page 149 |

Introducing Strategies

One way good readers respond to a poem is to read it in its **cultural context**. To do this, readers look for background information about the poet. They also note clues to the poet's culture in the work. Then good readers respond to the poem by comparing the poet's beliefs, experiences, and traditions to their own.

Study the diagram below, which shows how you can respond to a poem in its cultural context.

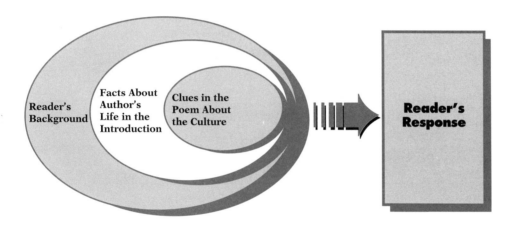

Reading the Poems

Read the poems "Leaves" and "Thirst" on pages 143-145 and then answer the questions below. Make sure you read the introduction to each poem as well as the sidenotes. These notes show how one good reader responded to each poem in its cultural context.

1. The reader learned in the introduction to "Leaves" that the poet's father was from the Middle East. Which word in line 2 of the poem is a clue to the poet's cultural background?
grapeleaves

2. How will knowing that the poet is Native American affect the reader's response to "Thirst"?
Accept any reasonable response that acknowledges Native Americans' respect for and

connection to the natural world.

Lesson Objective: To use a multi-level strategy for identifying clues to culture in the poems "Leaves," "Thirst," "Lineage," and "Incident."

Prior Knowledge: Locate Lebanon on a map. Point out other Middle Eastern countries and ask students what they know about the Middle East. Ask a volunteer to identify New Mexico on a map of the United States. Tell students that the poets whose work they are going to read are from Lebanon and New Mexico.

Cultural Awareness: Have students identify and briefly discuss their own cultural backgrounds.

Modeling the Strategy: Using the Reproducible Activity Master on page T16 of the ATE, show students how each of the elements shown can influence a reader's response to a poem.

Managing the Lesson: Remind students to carefully read the sidenotes on pages 143 and 145 as they read the poems. The sidenotes model the process of active reading.

Practicing Cultural Context

Purpose: The purpose of the **Practicing** page is to help students practice identifying cultural influences in poetry. Questions reflect the strategy illustrated in the graphic organizer on the **Introducing** page.

Individualized Learning: Have students complete the page independently. Make sure their explanations for section A support the items they have circled.

A. The following questions are about the poems "Leaves" and "Thirst" on pages 143-145. Circle the letter of the best answer for each question. Then give some evidence to support your choice.

1. Where are the best places to find clues to the poet's culture while reading "Leaves"?
   a. In the title and the first line
   b. In the introduction
   c. In the poem
   (d) In both b and c above

   Students may mention details from the introduction, as well as *grapeleaves, Arabic* _____

   letters and *grammar book*, and English lettering being hard for his father to print. _____

2. Which of the following details about the authors' cultural heritages may affect a reader's responses to the poems?
   (a) Native Americans believe things in nature are our brothers and sisters.
   b. The grape leaves are five years old.
   c. Hamod's father was a Muslim leader.
   d. a and c above.

   Students may suggest that the narrator in "Thirst" personified thirst, rain, and _____

   thunder. _____

3. Which of the lines from "Thirst" does *not* reflect the poet's Native American heritage?
   a. "At the male voice of thunder"
   b. "Over the nearest butte"
   (c) "What's that, over a distance?"
   d. "Spread your arms as to worship"

   Students may suggest the question reflects nothing; it simply asks what's over there. _____

   _____

Writing Process: Students might want to include recipes for the dishes they describe. Invite them to compile a cookbook that illustrates the cultural diversity of the class.

B. In "Leaves," the speaker is preparing a dish from his father's culture. Describe one of your favorite dishes and tell why you like it.

Accept all appropriate responses. Students should include details that connect their _____

feelings about the food with those of their cultural background. _____

_____

_____

Applying *Cultural Context*

A. Read the introduction and the poem below. Read the poem a second time and look for clues to its cultural context. Then complete the items that follow.

Leroy V. Quintana (1944-), born in Albuquerque, New Mexico, has often spoken about his fascination for the old stories (cuentos), which his grandfather and grandmother would tell, that combined his Chicano heritage and Native American traditions.

from "Legacy II"
by Leroy V. Quintana

Grandfather never went to school
spoke only a few words of English
a quiet man; when he talked
talked about simple things

planting corn or about the weather
sometimes herding sheep as a child.
One day pointed to the four directions
taught me their names

> *El Norte*
> *Poniente   Oriente*
> *El Sud*

1. List some facts in the introduction that provide important background information about the author's culture.

Chicano heritage; Mexican and Native American traditions

_____

_____

2. List some words or phrases in the poem that are clues to the grandfather's way of life and his culture.

He never went to school; only spoke a few words of English; quiet man; planting and

sheepherding

B. Compare the grandfather's way of life described in the poem to modern city life. Base your comparison on the first stanza of the poem. Use a separate sheet of paper to develop your paragraph.

Applying Skills to Everyday Reading: Students can practice relating the cultural background of the authors of books they read for pleasure.

Peer Sharing: Have students complete section A with a partner and work together to look for clues.

Conferencing: For part B, allow students to work with a peer to write their comparisons.

To review
page **148**

Author's Tone

| Lesson 16 | Introducing page 140 | Practicing page 141 | Applying page 142 | Reviewing page 150 | Testing page 151 |

Lesson Objective: To understand the importance of tone in response to the poems "Leaves," "Thirst," "Lineage," and "Incident."

Oral Language: Discuss with students how the tone of someone's voice can add to the meaning of words. Use a simple sentence, such as "Please shut the door," as an example.

Modeling the Strategy: Read aloud one of the poems from students' text to model identifying author's tone. Refer to the steps in the diagram. Use the Reproducible Activity Master on page T12 of the ATE to help students apply the strategy to the poem.

Managing the Lesson: Remind students to write their own sidenotes as they reread the poems.

Introducing Strategies

Tone is the author's attitude toward the subject of a piece of writing. The tone of a poem, story, or play can be humorous or serious, formal or informal, respectful or playful. Writers use tone to help get across their message to the reader. To figure out tone, good readers look closely for clue words that reveal the author's attitude. Then they respond to the clues and relate them to the author's message.

The diagram below shows a process for responding to the author's message and to the tone of a piece of writing.

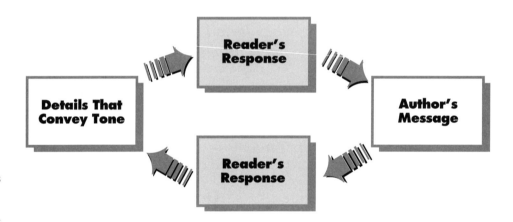

Reading the Poems

Reread the poems "Leaves" and "Thirst" on pages 143-145. Underline words and phrases in each poem that help convey the tone. Then follow the directions below.

1. List words or phrases in each poem that helped you identify the tone of the poem.

Accept all appropriate responses that illustrate students' understanding of tone. For

example, students might underline the words *carefully* and *making sure they didn't*

break into pieces from "Thirst," which illustrate the author's gentle, reminiscent tone.

2. Describe your responses to the words that you listed.

Accept all appropriate responses. Students should give details that support their

descriptions and increase their understanding of the author's message.

Practicing **Author's Tone**

A. Circle the letter next to the words that best answer each question. On the lines provided, write why you made the choices you did.

1. The tone of "Leaves" might be described as regretful. Which words from the poem convey this feeling?

    a. *it's one of the last things*

    b. *I keep this small torn record*

    c. *though it seems so late*

    (d.) a, b, and c above

The other choices are more sentimental, but accept any response students can

support.

2. Which sentence sums up the poet's attitude in "Thirst"?

    a. He is eager for his sheep to have a drink of water.

    b. He is nervous about the coming storm.

    (c.) He is joyfully preparing to welcome the rain.

    d. He is too thirsty to notice the weather.

His heart beat with joy; he opened his arms to worship the rain.

3. Which words are most helpful in determining the tone of celebration in "Thirst"?

    a. *distance, puffs, gray-shadowed clouds*

    (b.) *stormed with beats of joy, spread your arms as to worship*

    c. *thirst dried my smile, thunder*

    d. *stand still, placed a bucket*

The tone is one of joyful celebration.

B. In "Thirst," the speaker celebrates rain. Think about an event you enjoy celebrating. Describe the event, using words that create a joyful, excited tone.

Accept all reasonable responses. Students could describe their relationship to the

celebration, how they respond when celebrating, or what the celebration means

to them.

Purpose: The purpose of the **Practicing** page is to help students practice recognizing the tone reflected in poems. Questions follow the strategy illustrated in the graphic organizer on the **Introducing** page.

Peer Sharing: Suggest students complete section A independently. Then have them compare answers with a partner. Encourage students to make sure their partners provide details from the poems to support their answers.

Writing Process: Students might choose to develop their descriptions into the first draft of a poem.

Applying the Skill to Other Media:
Students can identify clues to tone as they read newspaper editorials, listen to songs, and watch the way in which television announcers report the news.

Cooperative Learning:
Have students complete the page in groups of three. One student could read the poem aloud, another moderate the discussion, the third record their responses.

Applying Author's Tone

Read the poem below. You may wish to make some notes in the margins about words that convey tone and the poet's purpose for writing. Answer the questions that follow.

> *They take me here*
> *They take me there*
> *In a long, gray car*
> *Which they think I*
> *need after winning*
> > *by chance*
> > *with a book*
> > *with a song*
> *They are wrong*
> *They do not know*
> *I did not want it so.*
>
> *I speak, agree*
> *my tongue polite*
> *while my mind rests*
> > *in a place quiet*
> > *and richer by far*
> *than in the long gray car.*

1. How would you describe the author's tone in this poem?

Accept any reasonable response that conveys the poet's tolerance to what others think

is important.

2. What words or phrases helped you identify the poet's attitude toward what is happening?

Responses may include: "Which they think I need," "they are wrong," "I did not want

it so," "my mind rests in a quiet place."

3. What do you think is the author's purpose for writing the poem?

Accept any reasonable response that suggests that a quiet place has more riches than

the trappings of wealth *or* that we can endure things we do not want to do by thinking

about something that is more agreeable to us.

To review

page 150

H. S. (Sam) Hamod (1936-) was born in Gary, Indiana. His father was an immigrant from Lebanon, a country that borders the Mediterranean Sea between Israel and Syria. Sam Hamod is a Muslim priest who has spent most of his life trying to improve communication between Muslims and Westerners. He has served as director of the Islamic Center in Washington, D. C.

Preteaching Vocabulary: You may wish to preteach the following vocabulary words: *butte, regretful, tolerant.*

Motivating Question: As students read the poems, ask them to think about how and why the poet's cultural heritage is important for the poet to express.

Leaves

by H. S. Hamod

Tonight, Sally and I are making stuffed
grapeleaves, we get out a package, it's
drying out, I've been saving it in the freezer, it's
one of the last things my father ever picked in this
life—they're over five years old
and up to now
we just kept finding packages of them in the
freezer, as if he were still picking them
somewhere   packing them
carefully to send to us
making sure they didn't break into pieces

"To my Dar Garnchildn
David and Lura
from Thr Jido"
twisted on tablet paper
between the lines
in this English lettering
hard for him even to print,
I keep this small torn record,
this piece of paper stays in the upstairs storage,

The notes on pages 143 and 145 show how one reader responded to "Leaves" and "Thirst" by noting the poets' backgrounds and identifying clues in the poems to the poets' cultures.

◀ Stuffed grape leaves. I know people from Greece and from the Middle East eat these. In the introduction it says the poet's father was from Lebanon—that's in the Middle East.

◀ Here he thinks about how carefully his father packed the grape leaves. That reminds me of my grandmother bringing homemade pasta over to our house.

Now write some of your own responses about the poet's background and cultural clues in "Leaves."

Meeting Individual Needs: If students have difficulty understanding what the poems say, have them follow along as you read each one aloud.

Response Clue: Underlining reflects words, which students may indentify, that convey the author's tone.

one of the few pieces of American
my father ever wrote. We find his Arabic letters
all over the place, even in the files we find
letters to him in English, one I found from Charles Atlas
telling him, in 1932,
"Of course, Mr. Hamod, <u>you too can build</u>
<u>your muscles like mine. . . .</u>"

Last week my mother told me, when I was
asking why I became a poet, "But don't you
     remember,
your father made up poems, don't you remember
     him
singing in the car as we drove—those were
     poems."
Even now, at night, I sometimes
get out the Arabic grammar book
<u>though it seems so late.</u>

ESL/LEP: Encourage students who speak a second language to share some of their experiences in learning a new language.

Making Predictions: You may wish to ask students if they think the narrator will learn Arabic.

Summarizing/Peer Sharing: Ask students to tell in their own words what the poem is about. Ask students to tell a partner which line or lines had the most meaning for them and why.

Grey Cohoe is a painter and a short story writer as well as a poet. He is a member of the Navajo Nation and was born in Shiprock, New Mexico, a town surrounded by desert in the northwest corner of New Mexico. This area is sacred to Native Americans, who believe that humans are a part of nature—that things in the natural world are our brothers or sisters, our mothers or fathers.

Thirst

by Grey Cohoe

What's that, over a distance?
White puffs of gray-shadowed clouds!

Thirst dried my smile—
Not as of sandstorm
Or grit of snow, but
As if it placed a bucket
And waited for a drink.

At the male voice of thunder
My heart stormed with beats of joy.

Slowly blue shadows spread
Over the nearest butte.
Rain approaches,
Wetting its path down the slope
Of our droughty land.

Are my sheep in?
No, don't bother to prepare!
Stand still,
Spread your arms as to worship.

Rain!
        Rain!
                Rain!

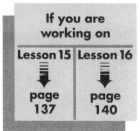

If you are working on

Lesson 15	Lesson 16
page 137	page 140

Margaret Walker (1915-) was raised in Birmingham, Alabama, attended Northwestern University, and later received her Ph.D. at the University of Iowa. Her poems are written in celebration of her people and in praise of their African American heritage. In addition to her highly praised poetry, she has written a novel, *Jubilee*, about the life of a woman born into slavery.

Lineage

by Margaret Walker

My grandmothers were strong,
They followed plows and bent to toil.
They moved through fields sowing seed.
They touched earth and grain grew.
They were full of sturdiness and singing.

My grandmothers are full of memories—
Smelling of soap and onions and wet clay
With veins rolling roughly over quick hands
They have many clean words to say.
My grandmothers were strong.
Why am I not as they?

Countee Cullen (1903-1946) was born Countee Leroy Porter. His birthplace and parents are unknown. Raised by a grandmother, he may have been adopted by Frederick A. Cullen, the pastor of a Harlem church. Cullen began publishing poetry as a high school student. His first book of poetry, *Color* was published in 1925, when he was 22 years old. Much of Cullen's work focuses on the subject of his African American heritage. He was a popular member of a group of African American poets who started the Harlem Renaissance, a movement named for the part of New York City where many blacks live. In 1930, when Cullen was on his way to a lecture, a restaurant in a train station refused to serve him.

Response Clue: Students may note details in the introduction that provide clues to the poet's involvement with his African American heritage.

Incident

by Countee Cullen

Once riding in old Baltimore,
    Heart-filled, head-filled with glee,
I saw a Baltimorean
    Keep looking straight at me.

Now I was eight and very small,
    And he was no whit bigger,
And so I smiled, but he poked out
    His tongue, and called me, "Nigger."

I saw the whole of Baltimore
    From May until December;
Of all the things that happened there
    That's all that I remember.

Use the margins to write your own sidenotes for the poem "Incident." In the notes, include how your own background affected your reading of the poem.

Response Clue: Students may note that "nigger" is a derogatory term. They may also note, however, that the word *glee* is a clue to the author's innocent and light-hearted tone.

ESL/LEP: Students may recall a time they were a victim of name-calling. They may note that this experience contributes to their understanding of and response to the poem.

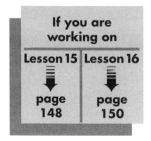

If you are working on

Lesson 15	Lesson 16
⬇	⬇
page 148	page 150

Incident ■ **147**

Reviewing *Cultural Context*

A. Read the poems "Lineage" and "Incident" and their introductions on pages 146-147. As you read, use the strategy for responding to literature in its context to write your sidenotes. Use the sidenotes to complete the diagram below.

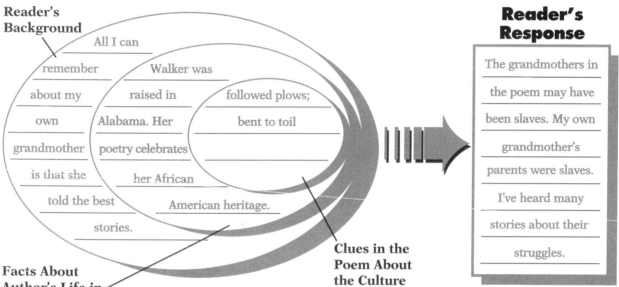

Reader's Background

All I can remember about my own grandmother is that she told the best stories.

Walker was raised in Alabama. Her poetry celebrates her African American heritage.

followed plows; bent to toil

Facts About Author's Life in the Introduction

Clues in the Poem About the Culture

Reader's Response

The grandmothers in the poem may have been slaves. My own grandmother's parents were slaves. I've heard many stories about their struggles.

B. "Incident" was written in the 1920s. Do you think what is described in the poem or something like it could happen today? Explain your response.

Accept any reasonable response that is well supported.

_____

_____

_____

_____

_____

_____

_____

_____

_____

_____

Testing **Cultural Context**

A. Only one item in each pair is correct. Fill in the oval next to the correct item. Then, on the lines provided, explain why you made the choice you did.

⬤ Information from the introduction for "Lineage" suggests that the grandmothers were probably African slaves in the United States.

◯ Information from the introduction for "Lineage" suggests that the grandmothers were probably from Lebanon.

The introduction mentions the poet's African American heritage.

_____

⬤ In "Lineage," the words through which Margaret Walker views the world are "My grandmothers were strong, why am I not as they?"

◯ In "Lineage," the words that show Walker's view of the world are "My grandmothers are full of memories."

She compares herself to people who she views as strong.

_____

◯ The title of "Incident" provides a clue to the speaker's ethnic background.

⬤ The only word in "Incident" that is a clue to the speaker's ethnic background is the name the little boy calls the speaker.

There are no other clues in the poem.

_____

⬤ Countee Cullen's poem can be read as an observation of how powerful bad experiences can be in our lives.

◯ Countee Cullen's poem can be read as a warning to the city of Baltimore.

One incident clouded his memory of a visit to Baltimore.

_____

B. In your own words, tell what the last two lines in the poem "Lineage" mean. How does it reflect the poet's feelings about her heritage?

Accept any reasonable response that suggests that the poet believes she does not have

the strength and courage that helped her grandmothers endure hardships she has not

experienced.

To begin
Lesson 16

page
140

Test-Taking Hints:
Remind students that only one item in each pair is correct. They should read through both items carefully before making a choice.

Meeting Individual Needs: Students may need to review the poems again or listen as you read them aloud.

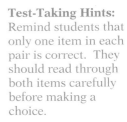

Reviewing *Author's Tone*

A. Read the poems "Lineage" and "Incident" on pages 146-147. Read the poems through another time. As you read, underline words that convey the author's tone. Complete the diagram below.

Reviewing the Strategy: Have students review the words they underlined before choosing one poem to use to complete the diagram.

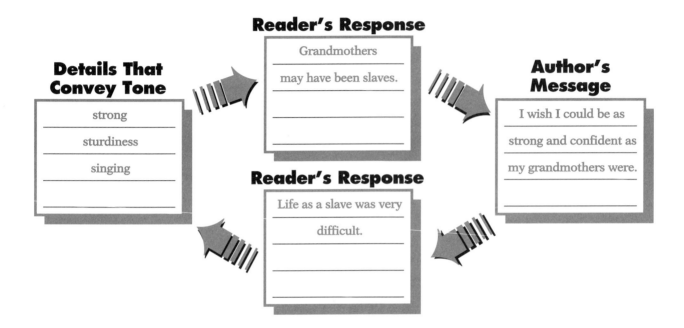

Details That Convey Tone

strong

sturdiness

singing

Reader's Response

Grandmothers

may have been slaves.

Reader's Response

Life as a slave was very

difficult.

Author's Message

I wish I could be as

strong and confident as

my grandmothers were.

Managing the Lesson: Answers on the chart are suggestions only. Students may find additional details that convey tone such as *quick hands, clean words*.

Conferencing: Encourage students to exchange papers to check each other's use of examples to support the response.

B. Describe the tone of the first ten lines of "Lineage." Then tell how the tone changes in the last line of the poem. Use examples from your diagram to support your response.

Accept all appropriate responses. Students should provide details from the poem to

support their answer.

_____

_____

_____

_____

_____

_____

_____

_____

_____

Testing Author's Tone

Test-Taking Hints: Remind students that only one answer is the *best.* They should remember to read all the choices carefully before marking an answer.

A. Circle the letter of the response that best completes each item. Then on the lines that follow, explain why you chose the response you did.

1. The tone of the first stanza of "Incident" creates a mood of
   a. mystery.　　　　　c. excitement.
   b. anger　　　　　　d. fear.

   The narrator said that he was filled with glee and that he was happy.
   _____

2. By the end of "Incident," the tone has changed. The author's attitude toward what happened is one of
   a. fury, rage.　　　　c. happiness, joy.
   b. sadness.　　　　　d. amusement.

   The incident blocked out everything else that had happened in Baltimore.
   _____

3. In "Lineage," the author's attitude toward the grandmothers is one of respect, pride, admiration, and love. Her attitude toward herself is
   a. not as positive.　　c. fearful.
   b. even more proud　　d. delighted.
   　　and respectful.

   She doesn't think she is as strong as her grandmothers were.
   _____

B. In your own words, explain the meaning of the last line of "Lineage." How does it reflect the poet's feelings about her heritage?

Accept all reasonable responses that are supported by details or examples from
_____
the poem.
_____
_____
_____
_____
_____
_____

Book Test

PART 1: FICTION

Read the story below. Draw circles and arrows to show relationships between key words and ideas as you respond to the story. Write notes in the margins. Then use the selection and your notes to answer the questions.

Another World

1 The flight from Seoul seemed endless. My interpreter had fallen asleep, apparently tired of talking about the United States. Now I was left alone with my own thoughts. The hum of the engine calmed the nervous feeling in my stomach.

2 I had lived in an orphanage in Seoul for as long as I could remember. Today at the age of fourteen, I was going to a new country to live with people who were strangers to me. I had met the Craigs, or "Mom" and "Dad" as I was to call them, at the orphanage. Although I knew some English, and they could speak a little Korean, it was difficult understanding each other. During the week that they visited me in Seoul, Mrs. Craig was always smiling and cheerful, and Mr. Craig always patted me on the back and talked about the ball games. We all felt more comfortable then.

3 My interpreter was to accompany me as far as the airport in New York. There, I would join the Craigs and travel to their home in Chicago, Illinois.

4 Illinois! At the orphanage, I found the state on a map of the U.S. It had a tall, thin shape and was near some very large lakes. The largest dot on the map was the city of Chicago. I closed my eyes and pictured the city that my interpreter had described.

5 I saw a large city filled with tall buildings and many cars and people. But would the roar of the Chicago streets be the same as the clamor in the streets of Seoul? Would I be able to smell the pungent odor from food vendors crowding the streets? Would I see boats gliding on the great lake near Chicago as I saw on the Han River near Seoul?

6 And what about the food? I was used to eating fish and rice, and my favorite Korean dish, *kimchi*. Would Mr. and Mrs. Craig be able to prepare this spicy mix of onions, cabbage, and other vegetables? I sure hoped so!

A. Circle the letter before the word or words that best answer each question. Ask students to provide evidence that supports each response.

1. Which words do NOT give clues to the point of view?
  a. I had lived
  b. patted me on the back
  c. the trip from Seoul
  d. we all felt
  point of view

2. Which words in paragraph 6 BEST describe *kimchi*?
  a. rice and fish
  b. onions and cabbage
  c. spicy mix of vegetables
  d. Korean dish
  context clues

3. Where is the narrator telling this story?
  a. in an orphanage
  b. on a train
  c. in Chicago, Illinois
  d. on an airplane
  making inferences

4. Which two words help the reader imagine noisy, citystreets?
  a. pungent, odor
  b. roar, clamor
  c. bright, gliding
  d. cold, hard
  sensory language

5. Which words are clues to the narrator's cultural background?
  a. Seoul, Korean, kimchi
  b. New York, Chicago, Illinois
  c. orphanage, interpreter, fourteen
  d. map, river, lake
  cultural context

6. How would you describe the tone of this selection?
  a. playful
  b. humorous
  c. serious
  d. mysterious
  author's tone

B. Imagine that you are the teenager in the story. Write a short poem describing your feelings. Use at least two sound devices. Your poem does not have to rhyme, but the sound devices should add special meaning to the poem.

sound and meaning

Students' poems should include words that reflect sound and meaning devices such as repitition, alliteration, rhythm, and sound words.

Book Test

PART 2: NONFICTION

Read the article below. Underline key facts and ideas and write notes in the margins as you read. Then use the selection and your notes to answer the questions.

THE THRILL OF AUTOMOBILE RACING

1 Auto racing holds a special place in the hearts of Americans. Each year, thousands of U.S. fans crowd tracks to watch their favorite type of auto racing. Whether the race is run on an oval track, a road-racing course, or a drag strip, spectators are guaranteed an exciting time!

The Tracks

2 Oval tracks have banked curves and long straight-aways. They are used in famous races such as the Daytona 500 and the Indianapolis 500. Driving distance on oval tracks can be less than 1/4 mile or as long as 2 1/2 miles.

3 Another type of track is the road-racing course. Road-racing courses look like country roads, with hills, straight-aways, and many turns. Sometimes road-racing courses are combined with oval tracks, or they may use actual roads as part of the course. In the United States, road-racing courses are usually between two and five miles long.

4 Drag racing is a special type of racing that emphasizes acceleration. The drag strip for this type of race is a straight surface on which two cars race side by side for just 1/4 mile.

Types of Cars

5 The types of cars used in auto racing are even more varied than the tracks. Indy cars are specially designed with an open cockpit, rear engine, and front and rear wings. Indy cars race on ovals as well as on road-racing courses. They use a special fuel called methanol because it does not catch fire as easily as gasoline.

6 Sports cars are racing autos with enclosed cockpits. Many sports cars are regular production cars that have been changed to make them lighter and faster. Stock cars are modified, American-made production cars.

7 Dragsters are highly specialized cars used in drag racing. Most have slim bodies with large tires in the rear. Dragsters also use parachutes to help them come to a stop.

A. Circle the letter before the words that best answer each question. Ask students to provide evidence that supports each response.

1. In what way are stock cars different from sports cars?

   a. They are production cars.
   b. They have open cockpits.
   c. They are lighter.
   (d.) They are American-made only.

compare and contrast

2. Which words are NOT key words related to the subject?

   a. tracks, courses, strips
   b. Daytona 500, Indianapolis 500
   (c.) thrill, fans, excitement
   d. drag racing, road racing

key words

3. What is the MAIN idea of paragraph 1?

   a. Auto racing is an exciting sport.
   b. There are many racing fans.
   (c.) Americans love auto racing.
   d. There are various kinds of race tracks.

main idea and details

4. Which statement states an opinion?

   (a.) paragraph 1, sentence 1
   b. paragraph 3, sentence 1
   c. paragraph 6, sentence 1
   d. paragraph 7, last sentence

fact and opinion

5. What is the BEST way to preview an article?

   a. search for important facts
   (b.) scan the title and headings
   c. look for reference
   d. scan for key words

reading encyclopedia articles

6. For what reason do Indy cars use methanol?

   a. It is less expensive than gasoline.
   (b.) It doesn't catch fire as easily as gasoline.
   c. It is the only fuel allowed.
   d. It makes cars run faster.

cause and effect

B. Imagine you are going to modify a normal car to make it into a fast stock car. Tell the sequence of steps you would take. In your writing, include signal words such as *first*, *next*, *last*, *then*, and *finally*. If you don't know much about cars, use your imagination. The steps in your writing can be as innovative or fantastic as you wish!

sequence

Students should use sequence words to describe how they might modify a normal car into a fast stock car. If they are being imaginative, they might install such inventions as a fusion-powered flux-capacitor, a matter-antimatter infusion device that feeds the hyperdrive, or some form of artificial intelligence. If they are being more realistic, they might add fuel injection, leather seats, a hood ornament, an unusual paint job, and a great sound system.